D0955998

TEN GREAT ENGLISH NOVELISTS

TEN GREAT
ENGLISH NOVELISTS

by

Valerie Grosvenor Myer

VISION PRESS · LONDON
ST. MARTIN'S PRESS · NEW YORK

Vision Press Ltd.
c/o Vine House Distribution
Waldenbury, North Common
Chailey, E. Sussex BN8 4DR

and

St. Martin's Press, Inc.
175 Fifth Avenue
New York
N.Y. 10010

ISBN (UK) 0 85478 027 0
ISBN (US) 0 312 03564 0

Library of Congress Cataloging-in-Publication Data

Myer, Valerie Grosvenor.
  Ten great English novelists/by Valerie Grosvenor Myer.
  ISBN 0-312-03564-0
   1. English fiction—History and criticism. I. Title.
PR821.M9 1990   89-77771
823.009—dc20   CIP

A CIP catalogue record is also available from the
British Library.

© 1990 by Valerie Grosvenor Myer
First published in the U.S.A. 1990

All rights reserved

Printed and bound in Great Britain by
Billing & Sons, Worcester.
Typeset by Galleon Photosetting,
Ipswich, Suffolk.
MCMLXL

Contents

Preface

The title of this book does not imply any kind of league table. I make no suggestion that these ten novelists, all British, all working in the eighteenth and nineteenth centuries, are the best or the only novelists; they are simply the ones for whom I have most sympathy. The choice was arbitrary, dictated by my own preferences; others would have included Defoe and Scott, Mrs. Gaskell and Trollope.

This is not a book for the expert. It is intended as an introduction to the great names of English literature for those who know little or nothing about them, but wish to fill gaps. Each section starts with a brief biographical introduction, and discusses those works which are still read today. There are many omissions. I hope to give some indication as to why the works I concentrate on are still considered worth reading. This book is no substitute for reading the novels themselves.

V.G.M.
Cambridge, 1989

1

Samuel Richardson: Father of the Psychological Novel, Who Made Novels Respectable

Samuel Richardson, novelist and printer, was born in 1689 and died in 1761. He was born in Derbyshire, but his father was a London joiner by trade, and the family had returned to the capital by 1700. Richardson would have liked to become a clergyman, but his father could not afford the necessary classical education. He was bound apprentice to a printer in 1706. Richardson did not enjoy his early years and all his life resented his lack of Latin and Greek, the acquirements of the gentleman of leisure and the professional man. In a letter to Johannes Sinstra, a Dutch reader, he writes:

> I served a diligent seven years to it, to a master who grudged every hour to me, that tended not to his profit, even of those times of leisure and diversion, which the refractoriness of my fellow-servants *obliged* him to allow them, and were usually allowed by other masters to their apprentices. . . . I stole from the hours of rest and relaxation, my reading times for the improvement of my mind . . . even my candle was of my own purchasing.

Uncongenial as this life was, Richardson made the best of it. Hardworking and highly intelligent, he did well. He married Martha Wilde, his master's daughter, in 1721, the year he set up in business by himself. He was 32, well-married and starting out on his own in life. By this first wife he had

9

five sons and one daughter, all of whom died young. This terrible grief affected his health. After the death of Martha, he married Elizabeth Leake, daughter of a fellow printer and sister of a bookseller. Elizabeth survived her husband. They had five girls and a boy, of whom four daughters survived.

In 1723 he took over the printing of the *True Briton*, an important Tory journal, and by 1727 was appointed Renter Warden of the Stationers' Company. Until the age of 50, he was a quietly successful tradesman. But the novelist's imagination had always been part of him. He was fascinated by the passion of love, and the secrets of the feminine heart. As a boy, Richardson—whose nicknames were 'Serious' and 'Gravity'—entertained his schoolfellows with tales remembered from his wide reading, and all his stories, or so he tells us, 'carried with them . . . a useful moral'. He served an unofficial apprenticeship, from the age of 13 onwards, to the trade of novel-writing by writing love-letters for illiterate servant girls.

> I have been directed to chide, and even repulse, when an offence was either taken or given, at the very moment when the heart of the chider or repulser was open before me, overflowing the esteem and affection; and the fair repulser dreading to be taken at her word. . . .

Before that he had sent a reproving letter to a lady who professed religion, but practised slander and backbiting. While still in his teens he provided prefaces and dedications for booksellers. In 1733, he published *The Apprentice's Vade Mecum*, which urged the ambitious youth to diligence, sobriety, self-denial and morality, an ethic of deferred gratification. These habits of life had worked for him, indeed, so that he had succeeded in winning every apprentice's dream-prize—the hand of his master's daughter. Richardson followed up his guide to useful conduct on the part of apprentices by rewriting *Aesop's Fables*, in his own version, emphasizing the morals. He also edited *The Negotiations of Sir Thomas Roe in his Embassy to the Ottoman Port for the years 1621 to 1628 Inclusive* (1740) and continued Daniel Defoe's *A Tour Through the Whole Island of Great Britain*, which was eventually completed anonymously.

Richardson prospered, and as well as his business address

off Fleet Street had other properties, first near Hammersmith, and later near Parsons Green. In 1754 he was elected Master of the Stationers' Company, and in 1760 he purchased a share of the patent of the printer to the king. He was highly strung and sensitive, and his success in life had been achieved at great personal cost: the brilliant boy had been too poor to receive the education he hankered for, and he had worked almost fanatically hard in order to succeed. Richardson's success was unusual. Unlike other novelists, he was not a professional man with a university education behind him. Tobias Smollett (1721–71), trained at Glasgow University, was a doctor, Henry Fielding (1707–54), educated at Eton College, was a lawyer, and Lawrence Sterne (1713–68), educated at Jesus College, Cambridge, was a clergyman. Richardson was a middle-class craftsman and tradesman, in a lower social position than any of theirs. But his work as a printer took him into the company of people better educated than himself. He printed the *Journals* of the House of Commons. His virtues were those of the industrious apprentice; his weakness was agreed to be his vanity. However, he was a self-made man, who started life with few advantages, and his achievement was distinguished. Among his circle of friends and admirers were two sisters, Lady Bradshaigh and Lady Echlin, both of whose correspondence with Richardson survives.

He became famous by writing three novels, starting with *Pamela* in 1740, consolidating his success with his masterpiece *Clarissa* in 1747–48, adding *Sir Charles Grandison* in 1753–54. All three novels are written as a series of letters. Though he did not invent the epistolary form, Richardson did invent the novel of everyday life, explicitly rejecting the 'improbable and the marvellous'. Taking a hint from his friend Samuel Johnson, the maker of Johnson's Dictionary, poet and biographer, Richardson also published *A Collection of the Moral and Instructive Sentiments, Maxims, Cautions and Reflections, Contained in the Histories of Pamela, Clarissa and Sir Charles Grandison, Digested Under Proper Heads* (1755).

The mockery of the Etonian novelist Henry Fielding was expressed in *Shamela* and *Joseph Andrews*, but otherwise Richardson's reputation during his lifetime stood high. Dr. Johnson's intelligent friend Mrs. Hester Thrale wrote in her commonplace book, 'Were I to make a scale of novel writers I should put Richardson first, then Rousseau; after them, but at an immeasurable distance—Charlotte Lennox, Smollett and Fielding.' Mrs. Thrale thought that both Fielding and Tobias Smollett 'knew the Husk of Life perfectly well', yet 'for the Kernel—you must go to either Richardson or Rousseau'. This was perceptive of Mrs. Thrale, for Richardson and Rousseau had invented the novel of psychological analysis. Samuel Johnson himself, though he admitted that 'if you were to read Richardson for the story your impatience would be so much fretted that you would hang yourself', believed that 'there is more knowledge of the human heart in one letter of Richardson's than in all of *Tom Jones'*.

Sir John Hawkins, however, is recorded by James Boswell, in the *Life of Dr. Samuel Johnson,* as despising Richardson. Hawkins described Richardson as

> a man of no learning, nor reading, but [he] had a vivid imagination, which he let loose in reflections on human life and manners, till it became so distended with sentiments, that for his own ease he was necessitated to vent them on paper.

By the end of the eighteenth century, Richardson's reputation was in decline. In 1797, when the feminist and rationalist Mary Hay was writing for the *Monthly Magazine,* she admitted he was 'a sovereign genius', but criticized his 'false and pernicious principles, the violation of truth and nature . . . absurd superstitions and ludicrous prejudices' and compared him unfavourably with Fielding and Smollett. During the nineteenth century, Richardson's supposedly effeminate preoccupations (his brilliant grasp of feminine psychology and his belief that chastity should be practised by males and females alike) were denigrated in comparison with Fielding's manliness. During the second half of the twentieth century, however, his greatness has been once more acknowledged.

He describes himself in a letter to his admirer, Lady Bradshaigh, at the age of 60:

> Short; rather plump than emaciated, notwithstanding his complaints: about five foot five inches; fair wig; lightish cloth coat, all black besides; one hand generally in his bosom the other a cane in it . . . looking directly foreright, as passers-by would imagine, but observing all that stirs on either hand of

him without moving his short neck . . . a regular even pace, stealing away ground, rather than seeming to rid it: a grey eye, too often over-clouded by mistiness from the head: by chance lively; very lively it will be, if he have hope of seeing a lady whom he loves and honours: his eye always on the ladies; if they have very large hoops, he looks down and supercilious, and as if he would be thought wise, but perhaps the sillier for that: as he approaches a lady, his eye is never fixed first upon her face, but upon her feet, and thence he raises it up, pretty quickly for a dull eye; and one would think (if we thought him at all worthy of observation) that from her air and (the last beheld) her face, he sets her down in his mind as *so* or *so*, and then passes on to the next object he meets: only then looking back, if he greatly likes or dislikes, as if he would see if the lady appear to be all of a piece, in one light or in the other.

Richardson's first novel, *Pamela*, published when he was 50, is one of the first important English novels. True, in the Elizabethan age there had been prose romances by John Lyly (*Euphues*, in two parts, 1578 and 1580) and Sir Philip Sidney (*Arcadia*, 1581), but the novel as we know it, a prose narrative about people in society, had hardly been invented. Although it has been frequently stated that Richardson could not have read widely, his work shows a detailed knowledge of Shakespeare's plays and of John Milton's verse epic, *Paradise Lost* (1667). The poem was essential reading for Protestants, as was John Bunyan's prose allegory of the Christian life, triumphing in death, *The Pilgrim's Progress* (1678). *Robinson Crusoe* (1719), was the most famous of Daniel Defoe's novels, though he wrote many works of fiction, including a *Journal of the Plague Year* (1722), which in spite of its circumstantial detail is pure invention. *Robinson Crusoe* is the tale of a shipwrecked mariner who survives by his own ingenuity and has been taken to be a parable of economic individualism. *Gulliver's Travels* (1726), a political satire which also managed to be the first science-fiction prose narrative in English, was widely known. The literary journal, the *Spectator*, published character sketches, but there were few models for Richardson to work with. Richardson was asked by two well-known publishers, Rivington and Osborne, to write a volume of 'familiar letters', partly for amusement, partly as models, for 'country readers' who, it was assumed, would not have much idea how to express themselves. And this turned into *Pamela*, in which a 15-year-old country virgin went to work for a squire, resisted his attempts at seduction, and finally succeeded in marrying her master. There is a story that church bells were rung to celebrate the marriage of the imaginary Pamela (the name comes from Sidney's *Arcadia*), because so many servant-girls identified with her. Whether or not it actually happened, the legend tells us something important about the way the tale was received.

Pamela is told in letters and journals, a form Richardson held to for his subsequent two novels. There were already various epistolary novels in existence, in English and in French, for example *Letters of a Portuguese Nun*, translated from the French (1678) and Aphra Behn's *Love-Letters between a Nobleman and his Sister* (1683), and the epistolary novel was associated, in the public mind, with dubious morals and titillation. *Pamela*, as its detractors were quick to point out, complied with conventional morality, but did not dispense with titillation. The story is told mainly by Pamela herself, in letters to her dear parents, Mr. and Mrs. Andrews, her employer, 'Mr. B.' having only two brief chances to express his point of view. Pamela has been employed by his mother, kind Lady B. When she dies, Lady B.'s son harasses Pamela with demands that she become his mistress (as would have indeed been normal at the time). Although Pamela finds him not unattractive, she resists. Mr. B. takes Pamela away from her friends, Mrs. Jervis the housekeeper, and Mr. Longman the steward, takes her from his house in Bedfordshire and locks her up in his remote house in Lincolnshire, B. Hall, where she is guarded by a human dragon, the harsh Mrs. Jewkes. Richardson makes Pamela use traditional imagery when Mr. B. says, 'So, Mrs. Jewkes, you are the wolf, I the vulture and this poor innocent lamb on her trial before us. . . .' He accuses Pamela of hypocrisy and Mrs. Jewkes tries to convince Pamela it is her duty to submit. Pamela's only comfort is from Mr. Williams, the family chaplain, but although he is sympathetic to her, he cannot affect Mr. B.'s conduct. For forty days of trial (which to the theologically literate reader recall Christ's forty days in the wilderness),

14

Pamela keeps a detailed journal, analysing her situation and her feelings. She sinks into despair, and even thinks of suicide, which in Christian terms is a sin (and was, until recently in England, a crime). In a passage which combines titillation, farce and transvestism, Mr. B. disguises himself as a woman servant, feigns illness and climbs into Pamela's bed, where he kisses her, while Mrs. Jewkes looks on. Mr. B. tells the girl she is in his power, but he does not force her, although he 'put his hand in my bosom'. Pamela conveniently faints away, and comes to herself to find Mr. B. looking concerned, although Mrs. Jewkes eggs him on to villainy. Pamela faints again and recovers to find a smelling bottle at her nose. Mr. B. is shamed into asking for forgiveness. Mr. B. imagines that he has broken her spirit by his harsh treatment, and, under the illusion that he is behaving generously, offers to make her his mistress and keep her in style. She refuses indignantly. She prays to be delivered from this 'Philistine, that I may not *defy the commands of the living God!*'

Pamela is warned, by an anonymous letter, that her employer plans a sham marriage. Then her employer comes and tells her he has intercepted her letters, and he accuses her of being in love with the clergyman, Mr. Williams. Mr. B. has a sister, Lady Davers, who despises him for running after a servant girl. Pamela writes about Lady Davers's letter to her brother, Mr. B., asking him to send Pamela back to her parents with some money. Pamela's comment on it is:

> This is a sad letter, my dear father and mother; one may see how poor people are despised by the proud and rich. . . . Surely these proud people never think what a short stage life is; and that, with all their vanity, a time is coming, when they must submit to be on a level with us. . . . These reflections occurred to my thoughts . . . and this proud letter of the *lowly* Lady Davers, against the *high-minded* Pamela. *Lowly*, I say, because she could *stoop* to such vain *pride*; and *high-minded* I, because I hope I am too proud ever to do the like!

Thus Richardson elevates moral virtue over pride of rank, which drew on him the scorn of the established classes of society. See the next chapter for Henry Fielding's satire, *Shamela*.

Eventually Mr. B. is won over by Pamela's firmness and her

sweetness and marries her. Pamela's unaffected goodness even overcomes the snobbish resentment of Lady Davers, and Pamela becomes a model wife and mother. The book was an enormous success, and there were various false and forged sequels. Richardson eventually supplied his own, but *Pamela II* lacks the vitality, variety and charm of *Pamela*. In it Pamela proves to be the perfect wife and perfect mother, wisely turning a blind eye to her husband's infidelities, bringing up her babies according to the educational ideas of the philosopher John Locke (1632–1704), then fashionable, and setting an example to all the other women of her husband's class by breast-feeding her own children, whereas they put theirs out to wet-nurse. The lively young Pamela has become a bore.

Soon after publishing *Pamela II* in 1741 Richardson started *Clarissa*, his enthralling masterpiece, a million words long. This novel, too, shows a woman in the power of a man who wishes to seduce her, but the ending is tragic, not comfortable. Richardson has been accused of vicarious sadism in his treatment of men who cruelly imprison and harrass women, but whether or not he shared the wish to dominate and destroy, he shows a frightening insight into the mind of the debauchee.

The plot, which only becomes clear towards the end of the second volume, is as follows: Lovelace, a handsome rake, who preys on women, loves them and leaves them, is courting Arabella Harlowe, Clarissa's elder sister. Lovelace is an aristocrat, whereas the Harlowes are rising gentry. Once again, Richardson's interest is in the struggle between different classes of society. The Harlowes are grasping and mean of soul, with the exception of the noble and talented Clarissa herself, a lovely girl of 18. When Lovelace sees Clarissa, he withdraws from his pursuit of Arabella, thus earning Arabella's undying enmity. Lovelace then starts making up to Clarissa. Aided and abetted by the jealous Arabella, Clarissa's parents, uncles and brother James decide that Lovelace is not rich enough for their family. James and Lovelace fell out when they were both students at Oxford University, and James wishes to spite Lovelace by thwarting his suit, while punishing Clarissa for being the favourite grandchild. James persuades the others that Clarissa must marry the wealthy but repellently ugly Solmes, whom she hates. James and Arabella are bitterly jealous that Clarissa, favoured by her grandfather, should have been left an estate of her own. She offers to give it up, but to no avail. Clarissa pleads to be allowed to stay single, but her relatives are intent on forcing her into marriage, in order to enrich the family, as her brother James is hoping for a peerage. She is locked in her room and snubbed by her relatives, who try to break her spirit, and threaten her with a forced marriage to Solmes. But as Lovelace himself tells us in a letter to his crony and fellow-rake, John Belford, the 'whole family are dancing on my wires'. By means of servants and letters left in the chink of a wall near the henhouse where Clarissa feeds her poultry, he and she are in communication. He tricks her into thinking that he is interceding with her family on her behalf, and persuades her that her only hope of escaping what she describes as Solmes's 'ugly weight' is to escape with Lovelace to London, where he promises her shelter. Although Clarissa recognizes that Lovelace has charm and wit and good looks, she is wary of his bad reputation where women are concerned, but in her desperation to escape a marriage with Solmes in her uncle's moated grange, she runs away with Lovelace. She has had her forebodings: she has a strange dream:

> Methought my brother, my Uncle Antony, and Mr. Solmes, had formed a plot to destroy Mr. Lovelace; who discovering it, and believing I had a hand in it, turned all his rage against me. I thought he made them all fly into foreign parts upon it; and and afterwards seizing upon me, carried me into a churchyard; and there, notwithstanding all my prayers and tears, and protestations of innocence, stabbed me to the heart, and then tumbled me into a deep grave ready dug, among two or three half-dissolved carcasses; throwing in the dirt and earth upon me with his hands, and trampling it down with his feet. . . .

This dream shows that Clarissa is afraid that she will be alienated from her family, and that Lovelace will both violate her and kill her (which in fact he does, indirectly). While Clarissa is still a prisoner at home, Lovelace promises to take her to his female relatives, but he takes her to a house of prostitution instead, the first of his betrayals. Lovelace is pursuing his own plan of revenge: he wants to punish the upstart Harlowe family for their pretensions and their rejection of him, and in planning to get the innocent Clarissa into his clutches he sets out to prove that all women can be seduced. The name 'Lovelace' is a pun on 'Loveless', and also denotes the eighteenth-century gentleman's love of finery.

Life at home was wretched enough for Clarissa, but she finds she has jumped out of the frying pan into the fire. Lovelace makes half-hearted proposals of marriage, but Clarissa says she cannot marry him or anybody else without the consent of her family. This may seem over-scrupulous to a modern audience, particularly as her reputation has been compromised by what looks to the world like an elopement; indeed, her family are convinced that Lovelace is her lover. At the time, to marry without the consent of one's parents was considered shameful indeed. Clarissa continues to hope for the impossible, reconciliation with her family; but they have given her up as a runaway, and look on her as ruined. Lovelace makes constant attempts to seduce her, and on one occasion he sets fire to the house in order to frighten her into his arms. Only her threat of suicide prevents him from sexual violence. Lovelace has been intercepting and tampering with her mail, and forging letters from his relatives to her. He also forges a letter from Clarissa's confidante, Anna Howe. Clarissa manages to escape to Hampstead, but Lovelace tracks her down, and persuades her landlady she is a runaway wife. Having got Clarissa to admit that she might, at one stage, have been ready to look favourably upon him, Lovelace says goodbye to his conscience, and decides she must be punished for running away from him and calling him 'an unchained Beelzebub' and a 'plotting villain'. He decides he must become her 'conqueror'. He tells Clarissa his relatives, Lady Betty and Miss Montague, will call upon her, but the pretended 'ladies' are London whores, easily seen through by the distressed Clarissa.

Lovelace takes Clarissa back to Mrs. Sinclair's brothel, which is a hell on earth, drugs her and rapes her. Lovelace, exhausted, reports, '. . . now, Belford, I can go no farther.

The affair is over. Clarissa lives.' Belford, in reply, calls his friend a 'savage-hearted monster', 'an implement in the devil's hands', 'the cruellest of men', and says that if he, Belford, had been Clarissa's brother, 'her violation must have been followed by the blood of one of us'. He tells Lovelace his conduct is 'barbarous villainy' on 'the most excellent of women'.

Clarissa, realizing what has happened, has a total breakdown. She escapes, but is arrested for debt. John Belford rescues her and takes care of her. He is moved by her virtue and sweetness to continue remonstrating with Lovelace. Lovelace half-heartedly writes about marrying her, but is all the time plotting infidelities when she has 'a young Lovelace at each charming breast'. He hopes he has made her pregnant, which would force her hand. Anna Howe repeatedly urges Clarissa to marry the man who has tricked her and raped her, but Clarissa is too proud. 'My soul is above thee, man!' she has cried, and she thereupon proves it by dying a Christian death, her main grief being that her family have repudiated her. She gives Lovelace false hope by writing to him that she is going to 'my father's house'. Lovelace imagines that reconciliation and even the marriage he is now anxious for will take place, but Clarissa means her Heavenly Father's house, not her earthly father's. She orders her coffin and keeps it at her bedside, as was the fashion at the time. She is repeatedly compared to an angel, and Lovelace to the devil. He has a dream in which she ascends to heaven in a spangled robe, which she drops as she goes. After her death, her cousin, Colonel Morden, comes from Europe and kills Lovelace in a duel. Lovelace's last words are 'Thus I expiate!'

After hearing of her death, he has lost all real interest in survival, but become obsessed with the idea of obtaining her pickled heart. Although *Clarissa* combines earthly tragedy with heavenly triumph, and Richardson's allegorical purpose held steady throughout, many readers, during the novel's serialization over more than a year, found Lovelace so attractive and witty a villain that they implored Richardson to let him marry Clarissa and make her happy, imagining that sexual harassment, psychological torture, kidnap and rape could be compensated by marriage. Lady Bradshaigh wrote to Richardson, 'I cannot help being fond of Lovelace. A sad dog! Why would you make him so wicked and yet so agreeable?' This is an unwilling compliment to the vitality of the character-drawing: yet Lovelace's letters make it plain that he is perverted. His goal is not, in fact, sexual pleasure (that is a 'bubble', he writes contemptuously), but power. He is driven by the lust of domination, and dreams of the 'glory to subdue a girl of family'. His attitude to sex is hateful: his letters are full of sly smut, and his idea of pleasure in relation to women is to degrade and humiliate them. D. H. Lawrence thought *Pamela* and *Clarissa* 'pornographical'. Lovelace is the heartless hunter of female hearts, Clarissa the victim who rises above physical violation to resist him and demonstrate her spiritual superiority. The letters reveal both events and the characters of their writers in subtle ways; only when letters are compared is it possible for the reader to understand exactly what has been going on, and the nature of Lovelace's double-crossing activities. Richardson skilfully demonstrates the man's wit as well as his wickedness, and the vacillations of Clarissa's responses towards him. In its subtle analysis of motive, *Clarissa* was a landmark in English literature, for Richardson was the father of the psychological novel. Part of his appeal to a wide audience was the way he showed the upper classes as corrupt, the lower classes as virtuous and religious. For a man of high abilities, pursuing a trade which made him a good living but denied him professional status, this was a comforting doctrine. Like his characters, Richardson might not be able to compete socially, but moral competition is open to all, even the humblest member of society. With the success of his novels, Richardson was able to have his cake and eat it: the lower middle-class printer became the writer of genius, flattered and courted by ladies of title.

His skill in dramatizing moral and psychological conflict ensured the success of *Pamela* and *Clarissa*. In his third novel, *Sir Charles Grandison*, however, such conflict as we find is not very interesting. The novel has its defenders and Jane Austen loved it; so did George Eliot, a century after it was written. Jane Austen writes in one of her letters about 'Harriet Byron's feather' and turned some of the book's incidents into family plays.

The heroine is Harriet, young, beautiful and charming. She dresses elegantly for a ball, with a feather drooping over one ear. She is kidnapped by the wicked Sir Hargrave Pollexfen, and rescued by Sir Charles, who is a model of all the virtues, the aristocratic hero as Christian gentleman. In addition, Sir Charles is an expert swordsman and always wins when he fights duels. Sir Charles and Harriet fall in love, but Sir Charles cannot wholly give his heart to Harriet; he is entangled with an Italian lady, Clementina Porretta, who is very much in love with him, but wants him to convert to her own religion, Roman Catholicism. Sir Charles, although agreeing that any children born to them will be brought up as Catholics, steadfastly maintains his own Protestantism, and Clementina's distress at this obstinacy, for she says she can never bring herself to marry a 'heretic', unhinges her mind. Unfortunately, the story, which Richardson was, by his own admission, never fully in control of, wanders into Italy, without his ever having been there or knowing a word of the language. The Italian characters talk in the same, emphatic, italicized fashion as those in *Clarissa*, and defy belief. Clementina's parents, desperate about their daughter's condition, send for Sir Charles, who leaves for Italy on the day Harriet realizes Sir Charles loves her as much as she loves him. Such small suspense as the novel holds is slung on this frail thread: which lady, both of whom love him, will Sir Charles choose? He seems, strangely, resigned to marrying either of them as fate decides. At the time, a man could not honourably break an engagement, or even an understanding: the lady had to 'release him' from it. Eventually Clementina recovers her mental stability, releases Sir Charles and declares she would like to become a nun, although her parents have found her a Catholic nobleman we are given to understand she may later accept. Harriet is finally rewarded for her long, anxious wait. Sir Charles is ready to make moral pronouncements, and relentlessly does so. It has been argued that the novel is an anthology of moral dilemmas, topics for debate, rather than a conventional narrative, but we tire of Sir Charles's honour, wisdom, courtesy and sexual piety. Sir

Charles too clearly represents an idealized, a fantasy self, for us to feel comfortable with him. Richardson was more successful writing about wicked seducers than about Christian gentlemen. Wicked seducers were a real danger; they either wished to marry rich heiresses for their money, or to seduce under cover of a mock marriage ceremony, performed by an unlicensed priest.

Richardson tried to create, in Sir Charles Grandison, a hero for us to love; but most readers ignore Sir Charles, in favour of Lovelace, the elegant villain we love to hate.

2

Henry Fielding:
Father of the Comic Novel

Henry Fielding, Richardson's great rival, was eighteen years younger, born in 1707 and dying in 1754. Fielding, unlike Richardson, was well-born, and went to Eton, England's leading public school. Fielding had the additional advantage of being six feet tall, in days when men were shorter than they are today, so he stood out. He was born at Sharpham Park, in Somerset, an old family seat. Among his school friends were William Pitt, the future Prime Minister, and Thomas Arne, the composer. Young Fielding construed (translated) Ovid and Homer, practised oratory on the models of the Roman Cicero and the Greek Demosthenes, and wrote verses in Greek. To Fielding were given the cultural treasures of Europe, which had been outside Richardson's reach. But the gain was not all Fielding's; there is no evidence that Fielding could match Richardson's detailed knowledge of literature in English, for English literature was not taught in traditional schools until the late nineteenth century. In those days a public school education involved Latin and Greek, and nothing else; there was no music or art, no mathematics or science, no compulsory games. He left school at about 16, and we know nothing of how he spent the next five years. He became a writer of plays, encouraged by his gifted cousin, Lady Mary Wortley Montagu. Then he went to university, belatedly, not to Oxford or Cambridge, as might have been expected, but to the University of Leyden, in Holland. There he pursued textual studies in the classics, and worked on the draft of a new play. He left the university, however, after eighteen months and settled in London. The population then was about 400,000; the crowded suburban areas we know today, such as Hackney and St. Pancras, were open fields. Fielding settled down to writing three or four plays a year. Aged 27, he married Charlotte Cradock, a beautiful girl who brought him a dowry of £1,500, useful for a struggling dramatist with aristocratic, expensive tastes and an insecure income. His own family money was tied up in inheritance lawsuits, as his father had married several times.

Fielding was successful, however, as a dramatist, until the Licensing Act was passed, bringing plays under the control of the censor. This was because the stage had been used as a vehicle for savage and obscene political satire. Henry Fielding realized that his precarious living would be even more precarious when the authorities could close down the performances which supported him, his wife and their two young daughters, living quietly in Salisbury.

Aged 30, following a family tradition, he started to train as a lawyer at the Middle Temple in London. The bohemian had been forced, by economic pressure, to turn conformist. His powers of concentration were admired by his friends. He needed all the application he could muster, for the course was ill-organized, indeed hardly organized at all. The student had only undirected reading and discussion as a means of learning. Fielding persevered and, unlike his fellow-students, many of whom were frivolous socialites idling their way along, he mastered a great deal of law. In 1739 he brought his family to live with him. His debts mounted. Within three years he was called to the bar, whereas most students took double that time. However, his good connections may have helped. His work meant long, tiring journeys on horseback or in slow, draughty coaches along bumpy roads, irregular meals and unpredictable judges. Judges and advocates alike were in danger of catching 'jail fever' (typhus) from prisoners in the dock. He was also writing editorials for a newspaper called the *Champion*, which appeared three days a week. This was an anti-government publication, attacking the unpopular Prime Minister, Sir Robert Walpole (who is also the chief object of satire, figured as the highwayman, Macheath, in

John Gay's *The Beggar's Opera*). Walpole's nickname was Bob Booty, as it was felt that not all his wealth could have been honestly earned. But Fielding gradually changed his views, and decided that the 'patriots' or left-wingers were no more than a wagon-load of aimless and mud-spattered travellers. He wrote a satire on them, called *The Opposition: A Vision*. His biographers think that the well-born, but struggling, young man could no longer afford the luxury of nonconformity. He had bills to pay.

In 1741 Fielding was far from prosperous. Richardson's success with *Pamela* had been prodigious: there were imitations, continuations, adaptations, dramatizations, panegyrical essays and pirate versions. Pamela's adventures were immortalized in paintings on a fan. There was a special waxwork exhibition. Sober clergymen like James Fordyce, who disapproved of novel-reading by young girls because novels painted 'scenes of pleasure and of passion', thought the novels of Richardson permissible, because they were so moral. Fielding, born a gentleman, did not agree that the book was moral. On the contrary, it could only encourage pretty servant girls in wild dreams of crossing class barriers and marrying their masters by prudence and guile. *An Apology for the Life of Mrs. Shamela Andrews* came out before Richardson could publish *Pamela II*. *Shamela* cuts poor Pamela down to size and shows her as a garrulous, conceited, scheming little hussy. Fielding pilloried the weaknesses of the novel: its occasional pomposity, its long-windedness, its artificiality.

Shamela went to three editions. It was published anonymously. A complication was that Fielding's sister Sarah, also a novelist, was a friend of Richardson's.

Fielding was not earning very much as a barrister. His darling daughter Charlotte died at the age of 5. Fielding started to suffer from gout. Soon Charlotte's brother Henry was born, but he too died at the age of 8. Grief and ill-health made it difficult for Fielding to work. In 1742 he published *The Adventures of Joseph Andrews and his Friend, Mr. Abraham Adams*, a story in which Pamela Andrews is given a brother even more virtuous than herself. His publisher paid him £185. 11s. for it, a considerable sum at the time. In 1743,

Fielding published three volumes of Miscellanies, including the ferocious satire, *The Life and Death of Jonathan Wild the Great*. But in 1744, his beloved wife died, a terrible blow. He took the children and went to live with his sister Sarah. A distant relative, Lady Louisa Stuart, wrote a century later, drawing on family tradition, that sometimes Henry and Charlotte

> . . . were living in decent lodgings with tolerable comfort; sometimes in a wretched garret without necessaries; not to speak of the spunging-houses and hiding places where he was occasionally to be found. His elastic gaiety of spirit carried him through it all; but meanwhile, care and anxiety were preying upon her more delicate mind, and undermining her constitution. She gradually declined, caught a fever, and died in his arms.

The death of their lovely little daughter cannot have helped. Fielding was inconsolable and his friends thought he was likely to go out of his mind. Fielding was unproductive for a while in the wake of this shock, and wrote only odd pieces of journalism and a preface to a novel by his sister Sarah, *David Simple*. In 1747 he married his wife's maid, Mary Daniel, who had wept for her mistress along with the bereaved husband. Indeed, she had consoled him for his loss in more ways than one, as at the time of her marriage to him she was six months pregnant. Here is a fine irony: the aristocratic novelist and lawyer who had mocked Richardson's story of a servant girl who gets so far above herself as to marry her employer, married a servant himself! He paid dearly for it, becoming the object of jokes, sneers and scandal. Class lines were rigid at the time. When, in 1745, Bonnie Prince Charlie led a Scots army southwards to claim the English throne for the Stuarts and Catholicism, Fielding was vociferously on the Hanoverian, Protestant side. After the rising was crushed at Culloden and Charles had fled back to France, the custom of singing 'God Save the King' at the end of public concerts arose.

With the help of friends, Fielding was appointed Justice of the Peace for Westminster in 1748 and attacked corruption in the legal profession.

When *Clarissa* appeared in 1747, Fielding was impressed.

Richardson sent him an advance copy, and Fielding generously wrote an enthusiastic letter:

> Let the overflowings of a heart which you have filled brimfull speak for me. . . . Here my terror ends and my grief begins which the cause of all my tumultuous passions soon changes into raptures of admiration and astonishment by a behaviour the most elevated I can possibly conceive.

He wished Richardson every success. Of the opening instalment of *Clarissa* Fielding wrote elsewhere: 'Such simplicity, such manners, such deep penetrations into nature; such power to raise and alarm the passions, few writers, either ancient or modern, have been possessed of.'

The History of Tom Jones, A Foundling, appeared in February 1749, and the first edition sold out immediately. By 1850 it had been translated into French, German and Dutch. One reviewer, however, described it as 'beneath the dignity of regular criticism' and a 'motley history of bastardism, fornication and adultery'. Samuel Richardson refused to read it, although all his friends recommended it. Racehorses were named after Fielding's books; there was even a race between a chestnut called Joseph Andrews and a bay called Tom Jones. Joseph won. After *Tom Jones*, Fielding wrote one more novel, *Amelia* (1751), which sold best of all his fictions, but he was now absorbed in writing legal pamphlets, including one which proposed that the practice of public hangings should be abolished. He was responsible for a plan which led to the smashing of criminal gangs then terrorizing London. Fielding's maternal grandfather had been a Justice of the King's Bench, but Fielding had made an indiscreet marriage and his career had been sporadic rather than steady. His health was ruined. He was asthmatic and could walk only with the aid of crutches. Another daughter was born to him, but she died in less than a year. Fielding's blind half-brother John was living in Fielding's home. In 1754, Henry travelled south in hope of better health. He was emaciated and dropsical: fourteen quarts of water were drawn from his belly, and the invalid was prescribed laudanum (an opium medicine). The miseries of this journey are recorded in his *The Journal of a Voyage to Lisbon*, published posthumously in 1755. Unable to walk, he had to be hoisted out of the little rowing boat into the ship.

I think, upon my entrance into the boat, I presented a spectacle of the highest horror. The total loss of limbs was apparent to all who saw me, and my face contained marks of a most diseased state, if not of death itself. Indeed, so ghastly was my countenance, that timorous women with child had abstained from my house, for fear of the ill consequences of looking at me. In this condition I ran the gauntlope (so I think I may justly call it) through rows of sailors and watermen, few of whom failed of paying their compliments to me by all manner of insults and jests on my misery. No man who knew me will think I conceived any personal resentment at this behaviour; but it was a lively picture of that cruelty and inhumanity in the nature of men which I have often contemplated with concern, and which leads the mind into a train of very uncomfortable and melancholy thoughts. It may be said that this barbarous custom is peculiar to the English, and of them only to the lowest degree; that is an excrescence of an uncontrolled licentiousness mistaken for liberty, and never shews itself in men who are polished and refined in such manner as human nature requires to produce that perfection of which it is susceptible, and to purge away all that malevolence of disposition of which, at our birth, we partake in common with the savage creation.

He died in Lisbon.

Fielding is generally agreed to be a great innovator. He described himself as 'the founder of a new province of writing', and Sir Walter Scott praised him for his 'high notions of the dignity of an art which he may be considered as having founded'. He wisely broke away from the epistolary convention, which enabled him to present an ironical view of his story through the words of his omniscient narrator. Fielding called his narratives 'comic epics in prose', and his are the first modern novels in English.

Fielding's novels are witty, allusive and learned; in the manner he learned from Jonathan Swift, they are oblique and ironical.

Shamela was published anonymously in 1741, In it, the gullible Parson Tickletext, overcome by the book, sends a copy to his friend, Parson Oliver, recommending 'sweet, dear, pretty Pamela'. He reports that at night he thinks about Pamela 'with all the Pride of Ornament cast off'. This is the first salvo in Fielding's attack: the book, he implies, is pruri-

ent and inflaming to men's imaginations. The letter continues
with wild praises, and the request: '. . . pray let your Serving
Maids read it, or read it to them.' In other words, Fielding is
saying, in reality, that servant girls should *not* be encouraged
to indulge in fantasies of marrying above them. Wickedly
Fielding catches Richardson's sermonizing manner. Parson
Oliver objects that the book is erotic: the reader sees 'the
Girl lie on her Back, with one Arm round Mrs. *Jewkes* and the
other round the Squire, naked in Bed, with his Hand on her
Breasts, &c.' Far from being respectable, says Parson Oliver,
Pamela was really called Shamela, her parents were low-life
characters and not married. Parson Oliver has letters which
show the squalid truth about the heroine, who has had a baby
by Parson Williams and is thoroughly deceitful. Shamela's
spelling and grammar are sub-standard. The events and the
characters are those of *Pamela*, but the moral viewpoint has
shifted: Parson Williams is a crooked schemer; Mr. B. has
become 'Mr. Booby'. Pamela is a calculating hussy, who
loves Williams, hates and despises Mr. Booby, but intends
to marry him for money, egged on by her mother, with the
collusion of Mrs. Jewkes. The novel of *Pamela* is made out
to be a whitewash job by a mercenary clergyman. The satire
is brilliant—and very cruel. Richardson never forgave it,
despite Fielding's sincere admiration for *Clarissa*.

Fielding continued the joke in his novel *Joseph Andrews,
The History of the Adventures of, and of his Friend Mr. Abraham
Adams* (1742). Its Preface is important, as stating Fielding's
aims, in

> . . . this kind of Writing, which I do not remember to
> have seen hitherto attempted in our Language . . . a comic
> Romance is a comic Epic-Poem in Prose, differing from
> Comedy, as the serious Epic from Tragedy; its Action being
> more extended and comprehensive; containing a much larger
> Circle of Incidents, and introducing a greater Variety of Char-
> acters. It differs from the serious Romance in its Fable and in
> this; that as in the one these are grave and solemn, so in the
> other they are light and ridiculous; it differs in its Characters,
> by introducing Persons of inferiour Rank, and consequently
> of inferiour Manners, whereas the grave Romance, sets the
> highest before us; lastly in its Sentiments and Diction, by
> preserving the ludicrous instead of the Sublime. In the Diction

I think, Burlesque itself may be sometimes admitted; of which many Instances will occur in this Work, as in the Descriptions of the Battles, and some other Places, not necessary to be pointed out to the Classical Reader for whose Entertainment those Parodies or Burlesque Imitations are chiefly calculated.

This extract alone demonstrates the difference in sophistication between Richardson, who had only his own talent and his knowledge of English Protestant literature, hortatory and confessional, to guide him, and Fielding, with his confident command of established critical terms and the ability to parody classical literature (which he delightfully does). He pleads for realism:

... from a just Imitation of [Nature] ... will flow all the Pleasure we can this way convey to a sensible Reader. And perhaps there is this one Reason, why a Comic Writer should of all others be the least excused for deviating from Nature, since it may not be always so easy for a serious Poet to meet with the Great and Admirable; but Life every where furnishes an accurate Observer with the Ridiculous. . . .

The only Source of the true Ridiculous (as it appears to me) is Affectation. . . . Affectation proceeds from one of these two causes, Vanity, or Hypocrisy: for as Vanity puts us on affecting false Characters, in order to purchase Applause; so Hypocrisy sets us on an Endeavour to avoid Censure by concealing our Vices under an Appearance of their opposite Virtues.

He defends himself against the charge that his work might be considered immoral:

... perhaps it may be objected to me, that I have against my own Rules introduced Vices, and of a very black Kind into this Work. To which I shall answer: First, that it is very difficult to pursue a Series of human Actions and keep clear from them. Secondly, that the Vices to be found here are rather the accidental Consequences of some human Frailty, or Foible, than Causes habitually existing in the Mind. Thirdly, that they are never set forth as the Objects of Ridicule, but Detestation. Fourthly, That they are never the principal Figure at that Time on the Scene, and lastly, they never produce the intended Evil.

Whereas the novels of Defoe had also been prose narratives, with first-person narrators, in the form of personal reminiscence, Fielding revived the omniscient narrator used by Homer in his two epics of the Trojan War, the *Iliad* and the *Odyssey*. Scholars are still arguing whether 'Homer' was one poet or several, but these epic poems, written from the Greek point of view, are consciously used by Fielding as models. The Greek epics celebrate a war won, and glorify their heroes, in particular their leader, Agamemnon, and the wily general, Odysseus, King of Ithaca. The *Odyssey* tells of his ten years of wandering around the Mediterranean sea as he tries to return home to his wife, Penelope. These epics deal solemnly with man's relation to the gods and the destinies they control. These epics, together with the Jewish Old Testament and the Christian New Testament, which together make up the Bible, are the roots of Western literary culture.

The great European prose innovator was Cervantes. While there were strolling story-tellers aplenty, Cervantes invented the comic novel and the novel as self-conscious genre. His *Don Quixote* is the precursor of multitudinous fictions in which the protagonist fails to distinguish between romance and reality (a prime example is Jane Austen's *Northanger Abbey*).

Fielding set out to tell a story, then, which would amuse the reader by its satire on affectation, and which would be morally sane. These criteria have been dominant in the English mainstream novel for two and a half centuries; most English novels, even those with tragic incidents, have humorous episodes.

The History of the Adventures of Joseph Andrews, and of his friend Mr. Abraham Adams, Written in Imitation of the Manner of Cervantes, Author of Don Quixote, continues its parody of Richardson's *Pamela.* Joseph is Pamela's brother, who at the age of 10 becomes stable-boy to Sir Thomas Booby. Eventually Joseph falls in love with Fanny the milkmaid, becomes footman to Sir Thomas and Lady Booby, and, together with Mrs. Slipslop the chambermaid, attends them for their season in London. Throughout Fielding draws attention to the structure of his novel and to its necessary artifice: for example, the heading to Chapter Eight reads, 'In which, after some very fine Writing, the History goes on, and relates the Interview between the Lady and Joseph. . .'. When Sir Thomas Booby dies, Joseph's employer, the widowed Lady Booby, makes amorous advances to him, which he virtuously rejects. The reader is expected to recognize the allusion to the Biblical story of the Israelite Joseph in Egypt, who resisted the advances of Potiphar's wife. Joseph is given the sack. His sister Pamela lives at the home of young squire Booby, nephew to Sir Thomas. Parson Adams, poor, learned and innocently convinced that everybody is as kind and generous as himself, takes a fatherly interest in Joseph. Fielding's constant theme is anxiety for the survival of goodness in this wicked world. Joseph sets out on foot to return to the family seat of the Boobys in Somerset, but is robbed and stripped naked, which is doubly awkward, as the night is cold and the clothes are borrowed. The naked Joseph is thrown into the ditch. The Christian parable of the Good Samaritan is invoked here. A coach passes, and when the postillion hears a groan, he investigates and reports that a naked man is sitting upright in the ditch. The lack of Christian charity is graphically illustrated:

> 'O *J-sus*,' cry'd the Lady. 'A naked Man! Dear Coachman, drive on and leave him.' At this the Gentleman got out of the Coach; and *Joseph* begged them, 'to have Mercy upon him: For that he had been robbed, and almost beaten to death.' 'Robbed,' cries an old Gentleman; 'Let us make all the haste imaginable, or we shall be robbed too.' A young Man, who belonged to the Law answered, 'he wished they had past by without taking any Notice: But that now they might be proved to have been *last in his Company*; if he should die, they might be called to some account for his Murther. He therefore thought it adviseable to save the poor Creature's Life, for their own sakes, if possible; at least, if he died, to prevent the Jury's finding *that they fled for it*. He was therefore *of Opinion*, to take the Man into the Coach, and carry him to the next Inn.' The Lady insisted, 'that he should not come into the Coach. That if they lifted him in, she would herself alight: for she had rather stay in that Place to all Eternity, than ride with a naked Man.'

The argument continues, while Joseph stands 'bleeding and shivering with the Cold'. Everybody argues from selfish motives, and no compassion is shown, though eventually the lawyer's prudent motives win the day: his argument is based on Giles Jacob, *A New Law Dictionary*, 1739 edition: '. . . it is held, that when one indicted of any capital Crime . . . is acquitted at his Trial, but found to have fled, he shall notwithstanding his Acquittal, forfeit his Goods. . . .'

Joseph, seeing the lady cowering behind her fan, refuses to get into the coach unless somebody offers him 'sufficient Covering'. The rich and comfortable refuse to lend their clothing, but the Postillion,

> (a Lad who hath been since transported for robbing a Hen-roost) had voluntarily stript off a Great Coat, his only Garment, at the same time swearing a great Oath (for which he was rebuked by the Passengers) 'that he would rather ride in his Shirt all his Life, than suffer a Fellow Creature to lie in so miserable a Condition.'

Joseph is taken to the inn kept by Mr. and Mrs. Towwouse, where he runs into Parson Adams who is on his way to London. Parson Adams, who has six children, needs money and hopes to get his sermons published. However, this absent-minded and sweet-natured soul had forgotten to bring them, so he turns back with Joseph towards Somerset. The good parson rescues a girl from an assault in a wood, only to find that she is Fanny, on her way to look for her beloved Joseph. There is a farcical scene in front of a magistrate. Fielding's chapter headings continue to delight the alert reader: here we have 'A Chapter very full of Learning'.

The pattern set in the coach episode is repeated with variations: Fanny, Joseph and Parson Adams, travelling together, short of cash, are helped by people as poor as themselves, poachers and coachmen. They apply to the rich Parson Trulliber. This clergyman is one of English literature's great comic creations; unlike the scholarly and conscientious Mr. Adams, who practises Christian charity on a small income, Trulliber is a farmer six days a week and a parson only on Sundays. Under the impression that Adams has come to deal in hogs, Trulliber drags him off to the sties, where a pig knocks him over into the muck. Trulliber roars with laughter and sneers at Adams for his incompetent handling of pigs. Trulliber's hospitality is coarse and miserly. When Adams asks for a loan, Trulliber and his wife assume they are to be robbed. Trulliber refuses, on the grounds that Adams's shabbiness is a disgrace to the cloth, with the wonderfully inconsistent remark, 'I know what Charity is, better than to give to Vagabonds.' He threatens to fight Adams, who merely smiles and says he is 'sorry to see such Men in Orders'.

The party are almost destitute, when they are relieved by Mr. Wilson, a country gentleman who tells them the story of his life. These interpolated narratives are in the tradition of Cervantes. Mr. Wilson's story is about poverty, the iniquities of London life, the vanities of the playhouse, and a brief, but idyllic, marriage broken only by the death of his wife is plainly related to Fielding's own vicissitudes. He also tells them his baby son was stolen by gypsies.

After further adventures, the party returns to Booby Hall, where the amorous Lady Booby tries to get Fanny, her rival, locked up in prison. Fanny and Joseph are arrested (and convicted) on a charge of cutting and taking away a hazel twig.

But there is a happy ending: it turns out that Wilson is Joseph's real father (here we are reminded of the classical stories of Oedipus and of Perseus, as well as the 'long-lost father' tradition of intermediate romances), Fanny is Pamela's sister. Joseph and Fanny are married by Parson Adams, who is given a living with a much higher stipend than his previous inadequate one.

Mrs. Elizabeth Carter, the bluestocking praised by Dr. Samuel Johnson for being able to make a pudding as well as translate Epictetus, gave it high praise.

The History of Tom Jones, A Foundling, has a complicated, but coherent, plot. Mr. Allworthy, a kindly landowner, lives in Somerset with his embittered spinster sister, Bridget. Late one evening Mr. Allworthy finds a baby lying in his bed, a boy. He names the child Tom and adopts him, calling him Jones, because he has jumped to the conclusion that the mother is Jenny Jones. Jenny is a highly intelligent girl, maid in the family of the schoolmaster Partridge, and she has learned Latin from him. Her intellectual superiority makes her unpopular with people of her own class. Jenny, who has nursed Bridget through a night's illness recently, appears suddenly in a new silk gown and laced cap, and the worst is suspected, while Partridge is accused of being the father and sacked. Both Jenny and Partridge disappear. Meanwhile Bridget marries Captain Blifil, a peculiarly unpleasant person, and they have a son, Master Blifil.

He and Tom are brought up together by the chaplain

Thwackum and the philosopher Square. These two gentle-man polarize, with considerable wit on Fielding's part, views of life commonly held in the eighteenth century. Thwackum, as his name implies, beats the boys mercilessly. He is a traditionalist, even a reactionary. Mr. Thwackum, a clergyman, believes that human nature is deeply depraved and can only be improved by the divine power of grace. All his conversation is based on the scriptures and commentaries on them, without referring to common observation of life. He does not believe any morality is possible without religion, and to him belongs the magnificently bigoted declaration: 'When I mention religion, I mean the Christian religion; and not only the Christian religion, but the Protestant religion; and not only the Protestant religion, but the Church of England.'

His enemy, Mr. Square, does not hold with religion. Although of limited intelligence, he has read deeply in classical literature. Square believes that human nature is naturally good and that wickedness is a perversion of nature. Square believes in 'the natural beauty of virtue', the 'unalterable rule of right, and the eternal fitness of things'. Following the philosopher John Locke, he says it is 'impossible to discourse philosophically concerning words, till their meaning was first established', but he believes that the natural beauty of virtue can exist independently of any religion whatever.

Fielding's own position is made explicitly clear:

> I will say boldly that both religion and virtue have received more real discredit from hypocrites than the wittiest profligates or infidels could ever cast upon them; nay, farther, as these two, in their purity are rightly called the bands of civil society, and are indeed the greatest of blessings; so when poisoned and corrupted with fraud, pretence, and affectation, they have become the worst of civil curses, and have enabled men to perpetrate the most cruel mischiefs to their own species. . . . neither of these men were fools . . . Had not Thwackum too much neglected virtue, and Square, religion, . . . and had not both utterly discarded all natural goodness of heart, they had never been represented as the objects of derision. . . .

Neighbours to the Allworthy family are Squire Western, an unforgettable comic creation, who hunts the fox, talks dialect, is loutish and outrageous, yet in his unthinking vitality a truthful and vivid portrait. Mr. Allworthy has a gamekeeper, Black George Seagrim, who has daughters.

Throughout childhood, Tom is straightforward and Blifil sly. Tom gets punished for small misdemeanours, whereas Blifil preserves by deceit the good opinion of his elders.

At 19, Tom falls in love with Squire Western's beautiful daughter Sophia, whose only amusement is playing music to her father in the evenings. He is determined to marry her to Blifil, although there are larger estates in the county:

> . . . and I had rather bate something, than marry my daughter among strangers and foreigners. Besides, most o' zuch great estates be in the hands of lords, and I heate the very name of *themmun*.

Blifil, unlike the illegitimate Tom, is heir to the estate next door to Squire Western's, and Blifil bears a good character. Tom meanwhile, trying to help Black George, comes across and has an affair with Molly, Black George's daughter, in whose bedroom the philosopher Square is also discovered. Thanks to intrigue on the part of Blifil, Tom is thrown out of the house by Allworthy.

Sophia, unwilling to be married to Blifil at her father's command, also runs away with her maid Honour, hoping to find refuge with Lady Bellaston, to whom she is related, in London.

Tom has various adventures on the road, and his original plan of going to sea is affected by his meeting a party of redcoats. The events of the 1745 Jacobite rebellion, led by Bonnie Prince Charlie, the Young Pretender, are interwoven with the narrative. Tom comes across Partridge, now reduced to travelling the country as a barber-surgeon. Unknown to Tom, he and Sophia fetch up in the same inn at Upton, where Tom goes to bed with a Mrs. Waters. Partridge leads Sophia to believe that Tom no longer loves her, and the distressed girl rushes on towards London. Tom follows her, and in London finds himself involved in an affair with the rich Lady Bellaston, who supplies him with the means to live. Lady Bellaston's friend Lord Fellamar has designs on Sophia, and they prevent Tom from seeing her, but Squire

Western arrives and puts a stop to Fellamar's plans. Partridge explains that 'Mrs. Waters' is actually Jenny Jones, and Tom is horrified to think that he has been to bed with his own mother. But Jenny explains that Tom's mother was really Bridget Allworthy, who has died and confessed everything to her brother before her demise. Tom's father was a man who died young. Lady Bellaston and Lord Fellamar, wishing to get rid of Tom, try and have him taken by the press-gang. This organization kidnapped men in order to make them serve in the navy (gentlemen born were exempt, but common people went in fear of being hi-jacked and sent to sea). But Tom gets involved in a fight, and apparently kills his attacker. Sophia is horrified to hear that Tom has been sleeping with Lady Bellaston, old enough to be his mother. Blifil intrigues once more against Tom, but Tom is rescued by Square, who writes a long letter to Allworthy, explaining that Tom has 'the noblest generosity of heart, the most perfect capacity for friendship, the highest integrity, and indeed every virtue which can ennoble a man'. Square comes on his deathbed to religion, admitting that 'the pride of philosophy had intoxicated my reason'. Tom has been 'basely injured'. Tom is thus rehabilitated in the eyes of his guardian. Sophia forgives Tom, receives her father's blessing, and marries Tom, who forgives everybody.

Dr. Johnson thought the book 'corrupt', because of Tom's affairs before marriage, and Samuel Richardson made similar objections. However, Fielding's targets of satire are atheism, scepticism, fanaticism and egocentricity, and his doctrine is that of charity and compassion.

The story is allusive to classical and Christian literature, as always in Fielding. The name Sophia means 'heavenly wisdom'. Thwackum and Square are both improbable names: 'Thwackum' indicates what the character does; 'Square' is at first sight more puzzling. The square was believed to be the perfect figure, its four corners corresponding to the four points of the compass and the four cardinal virtues (justice, prudence, temperance and fortitude). The expression was used by Christian theologians, the medieval schoolmen, to distinguish the 'natural' virtues from the 'theological' virtues (faith, hope and charity), while to 'square the circle' was a proverbial phrase for an impossibility. Within the novel, the pretensions of the deist philosopher to 'perfect virtue' are exposed as hypocritical and absurd.

The association of virtue with the word 'square' is found in John Locke's *Essay Concerning Human Understanding* (1690):

> . . . it is as insignificant to ask whether man's will be free, as to ask whether his sleep be swift, or his virtue square. . . . Everyone would laugh at the absurdity of such a question as either of these. (Book II, Chapter 21, paragraph 14)

As well as taking from Locke's writings the name of his deist philosopher, Fielding drew on Locke's *Thoughts Concerning Education* for the moral basis of Tom's character. Locke writes:

> Having laid the foundations of virtue in a true notion of God . . . the next thing to be taken care of, is to keep him exactly to speaking the truth, and by all ways imaginable inclining him to be good-natured. Let him know that twenty faults are sooner to be forgiven, than the straining to truth, to cover any one by an excuse. And to teach him betimes to love, and be good-natured to others, is to lay the early foundations of an honest man: all injustice generally springing from too great love of ourselves and too little of others.

Tom himself says, '. . . though I have been a very wild young fellow, still in my most serious moments, and at bottom, I am really a Christian.'

The *Oxford English Dictionary* offers as definitions of the word 'square': 'solid, steady, reliable'. The philosopher of that name pretends to be these things, but without goodness of heart such pretensions to virtue are absurd. Tom is good-hearted and truthful; unlike Square, he is kind and generous. Fielding is testing the concept of 'virtue' and saying that sexual pecadilloes can be forgiven a young man who has the virtues enumerated by Locke and who is free of meanness, cant and hypocrisy, the vices of Square and of Blifil.

3

Laurence Sterne, Who Teased his Readers

Laurence Sterne, clergyman and novelist, was born in Clonmel, Ireland, in 1713 and died of consumption in 1768. His father was the grandson of an Archbishop of York and the second son of a wealthy and well-connected Yorkshire landowner, but like other younger sons he had to fend for himself. He was only an impoverished infantry ensign, the lowest of the commissioned ranks. Laurence was the only son to survive. Sterne was the second child. He and his older sister had an unsettled childhood, wandering from barracks to barracks in England and Ireland. This experience of army life sank deep into Sterne's personality, and was to emerge later in his portraits of Uncle Toby and Corporal Trim. He describes his father, in the *Memoir* written for his daughter, Lydia Medalle, as 'a little smart man—active to the last degree, in all exercises—and patient of fatigue and disappointments, of which it pleased God to give him full measure—he was in his temper somewhat rapid, and hasty—but of a kindly, sweet disposition, void of all design; and so innocent in his own intentions, that he suspected no one. . . .' Sterne's father was run through the body in a duel over a goose, in 1731. Aged 10, young Laurence went to school in the town of Halifax, Yorkshire, under the care of his Uncle Richard, who had inherited the family estate, and went on to Jesus College, Cambridge, on a scholarship founded by his great-grandfather, Archbishop Sterne, who had been Master of that college. Younger sons of good family went into the church, the army or the law: Richard, as the eldest, had inherited; Roger went in the army; and Jacques had gone into the church (he had become an influential ecclesiastical dignitary).

Poor Laurence already had tuberculosis. As a young man of education and family without means, he took the obvious course and followed his Uncle Jacques into the church. This uncle procured him a living, and in 1738 Sterne became the incumbent of Sutton-on-the-Forest, Yorkshire. Sterne lived, not in that village, but in the city of York, then the social capital of northern England. In 1741 he was promoted to become a prebendary of York Cathedral, which was not an onerous post, as all it needed was to preach occasionally in the cathedral. And it made him good social contacts. That same year he married Elizabeth Lumley, a member of the minor county gentry. Sterne told his daughter:

> One evening that I was sitting by her with an almost broken heart to see her so ill, she said, 'My dear Lawrey, I can never be yours, for I verily believe I have not long to live—but I have left you every shilling of my fortune'; upon that she shewed me her will—this generosity overpowered me. It pleased God that she recovered, and I married her in the year 1741.

Unfortunately, Elizabeth Lumley and Sterne were miserable together. She was extravagant, unattractive and subject to mental disturbance. In certain moods she fancied she was 'the Queen of Bohemia', a fancy not so absurd as it sounds, as Bohemia is the name of a district in Lincolnshire. They quarrelled constantly, but had several children, of whom only their daughter, Lydia, survived. Sterne, however, living quietly at Sutton, where he used his wife's dowry to improve the parsonage, tried his hand at farming. He got on in the world: he became a Justice of the Peace, was respected as a priest, and admired as a preacher. In 1744 he gained an additional living, that of Stillington, the next parish to Sutton, which meant a double stipend. He had several ways of relaxing: he went riding, hunting, fishing and skating; he was an amateur painter and both he and his wife were good musicians. He played the violin. He could read Greek, Latin, French and Italian, was attracted by curious learning.

He kept up a friendship, begun at college, with John

Hall-Stevenson, who owned Skelton Hall (nicknamed 'Crazy Castle'), where drunken orgies were frequent.

Sterne quarrelled with his Uncle Jacques, who blackened his character. Then he got into hot water in 1759, with *A Political Romance*, a sharp satire on a quarrel between Dean Fountayne and Dr. Francis Topham, a York lawyer, as to who should have the lucrative office of Commissary of the Exchequer and Prerogative Courts. Dr. Topham tried to secure the post for his son, who was still a child. Dean Fountayne, who was a friend of Sterne's, put a stop to such shameless corruption. The row became public and Sterne satirized the whole affair, pretending it was a petty parish squabble. Dr. Topham becomes 'Trim the sexton', whose duty is whipping the dogs, and the author labels his emaciated self as 'Lorry Slim'. 'Trim', after a long career of grabbing all the local privileges for himself, asks the parson for an 'old watch-coat' to turn into a *'warm Under-Petticoat* for his wife and a *Jerkin* for himself'.

However, the celebrity/notoriety of this pamphlet gave Sterne confidence, although it had been burned after it was printed and was never distributed. That year Sterne put a curate in charge of his parishes and started to write the novel which has earned him immortality, *Tristram Shandy*. Sterne's avowed practice was that of 'writing the first sentence—and trusting to Almighty God for the second'. Poor Tristram throws, by mistake, 'a fair sheet, which I had just finished, and carefully wrote out, slap into the fire, instead of the foul one', and we may believe that Sterne must have made the same error, under pressure. The novel is deliberately random and formless, a commentary on the hopelessness of encapsulating the fluidity of life in the fixed form of a narrative. Early in 1760, Sterne, who said he wrote 'not to be *fed* but to be *famous*' found his ambition fulfilled, although the first two volumes had been rejected by the London printer Robert Dodsley (who suggested to Dr. Johnson that he might compile a dictionary). *Tristram Shandy's* first two volumes were published in York in 1759 at Sterne's own expense, and Dodsley agreed to take half the print-run to sell in London. Indeed Robert now offered Sterne £250 (then a large sum) for the copyright of the first two volumes and £380 for the copyright of the next two. Sterne became not only famous, but rich; but he was a dying man.

Sterne's relationship with his wife seems to have broken down, and at the time *Tristram Shandy* appeared, he was enjoying a sentimental friendship with Catherine Fourmantel, a singer who was at the time staying in York. Some people have identified her, but without sure foundation, as the 'dear Jenny' of *Tristram Shandy*. Sterne's latest biographer, Arthur Cash, has written of Sterne's fondness for such tender flirtations,

> He wanted love. He wanted it to be with gentlewomen, and he wanted it to be sweet, pleasurable and profound. And because he wanted it to be free of blame, even for a clergyman, he wanted it to be public. To supply these moral rather than sexual needs, he invented his own sort of sentimental love.

Sterne made do with the company of actresses. In a letter to John Hall-Stevenson, written in Latin, Sterne wrote: 'I am sick and tired of my wife more than ever—and I am possessed by a Devil who drives me to town.'

Sterne's friend and patron, Lord Fauconberg, offered Sterne a third living, at Coxwold, in Yorkshire. The parsonage was a rambling and beautiful house, now lovingly restored from ruin by Mr. Kenneth Monkman, the world's leading expert on Sterne. Sterne wrote the rest of *Tristram Shandy* there ('shandy' is a Yorkshire dialect word, meaning crack-brained). He also capitalized on his fame by publishing *The Sermons of Mr. Yorick* (in 1760 and 1766).

Sterne was petted and admired by society, was invited to court, painted by the portraitist Sir Joshua Reynolds, and published the second edition of Volumes I and II of *Tristram*. In 1761 the next four volumes were published. But poor Sterne's lungs were rotten, and he set off for the warmer climate of France with his wife and daughter, in search of health. In 1764, Sterne came back to England and wrote Volumes VII and VIII of *Tristram Shandy*, which describe travels in France. His wife and daughter settled in France, where Lydia was eventually to marry a Frenchman. In 1765, Sterne rejoined his womenfolk, and went on an eight-month tour of France and Italy, which gave him matter for his *A*

Sentimental Journey Through France and Italy (1768). Sterne was writing his *Journal to Eliza*, which he did not publish. Elizabeth or Eliza Draper (1744–78) was the young wife of Daniel Draper, an official of the East India Company. She followed her husband to the East, and Sterne wrote, as well as the *Journal*, the *Letters of Yorick to Eliza*. The ninth and final volume of *Tristram Shandy* had already come out. He died in London lodgings in March 1768. An eye-witness reports that he stayed conscious to the last: '. . . he said, "*Now it is come.*" He put up his hand, as if to stop a blow, and died in a minute.'

It is said that his body was snatched by grave-robbers, recognized by a friend when it turned up during an anatomy lecture in Cambridge, and reburied in London. Since then, what are believed to be his bones have been buried a third time, in the ancient burial ground of the church at Coxwold, where he served as priest, on its warm southern side. A skull with the top sawn off as part of the dissection process was measured with calipers and found to be compatible with the Nollekins bust. A special memorial service, attended by Sterne scholars from all over the world, preceded the interment.

William Makepeace Thackeray wrote that Sterne

> used to blubber perpetually in his study, and finding his tears infectious, and that they brought him a great popularity, he exercised the lucrative gift of weeping, he utilised it, and cried on every occasion. I own that I don't value or respect much the cheap dribble of those fountains. He fatigues me with his perpetual disquiet and his uneasy appeals to my risible or sentimental faculties. He is always looking in my face, watching his effect, uncertain whether I think him an impostor or not; posture-making, coaxing and imploring me.

While everything Thackeray says is tenable, one might argue that he misses the point. Sterne was concerned to write what actually passes through a man's mind, not what is supposed to. Sterne writes:

> If the fixture of *Momus's* glass, in the human breast, according to the proposed emendation of that arch-critick, had taken place,—first, This foolish consequence would certainly have

followed,—That the very wisest and the very gravest of us all, in one coin or other, must have paid window-money every day of our lives.

And secondly, That had the said glass been there set up, nothing more would have been wanting, in order to have taken a man's character, but to have taken a chair and gone softly, as you would to a dioptrical beehive, and look'd in,—view'd the soul stark naked;—observ'd all her motions,—her machinations;—traced all her maggots from their first engendering to their crawling forth;—watched her loose in her frisks, her gambols, her capricios . . .

But this, as I said above, is not the case of the inhabitants of this earth;—our minds shine not through the body, but are wrapt up here in a dark covering of uncrystalised flesh and blood; so that if we could come to the specifick characters of them, we must go some other way to work.

Momus, the god of fault-finding, is said to have criticized the work of Vulcan, blacksmith to the gods, on the grounds that man had not been made with a window in his breast, so that everybody could see his thoughts and whether he was lying or telling the truth. Sterne is making a pun on 'maggots', which in older English means 'fancies, whims, eccentricities'; he invokes here maggots which crawl forth from rotting meat, from the eggs of blowflies, and hints at graveworms. Sterne the consumptive, despite his laughter, is much possessed by sickness and death. Frail and emaciated, he was quiveringly sensitive to 'skin, hair, fat, flesh, veins, arteries, ligaments, nerves, cartileges, bones', that mortal clay of whose vulnerability and short lease he was, as novelist and clergyman, constantly aware. The passage also reflects Sterne's constant preoccupation as to what constituted human nature: what was the relation of the frail and sickly body to the mind, and the soul, which Sterne, as a Christian priest, was duty bound to consider immortal? He writes:

A man's body and his mind, with the utmost reverence to both I speak it, are exactly like a jerkin, and a jerkin's lining;—rumple the one—you rumple the other.

Here Sterne was, despite his use of older writers like Rabelais, Cervantes and Robert Burton, very much a man of his time, in emphasizing the interaction of mind and body. Scientific speculation was concerned with the nature of life itself, with fluidity, stimulus and response, pleasure and pain, the nature and limits of perception. Mid-century images of Nature tended to be interactive, dominated by flux and modification. Sterne saw his work as a remedy for life's ills:

> —True *Shandeism*, think what you will against it, opens the heart and the lungs, and like all those affections which partake of its nature, it forces the blood and other vital fluids of the body to run freely thro' its channels, and makes the wheel of life run long and chearfully round.

In his acceptance of tears as well as health-restoring laughter, Sterne was typical of his age: Fielding's Sophia, in *Tom Jones*, says she has enjoyed a book with 'so much true tenderness and delicacy, that it hath cost me many a tear. . . . I love a tender sensation . . . and would pay the price of a tear for it at any time.'

In a world where religion was in decline and science was gaining increasing prestige, people were asking what was the place of emotion? Ultimately the emotions and the imagination were to be endorsed in the Romantic movement. Sterne tries to capture the flux of thought and feeling, to escape the formal constrictions of the novel plot, whereas Fielding merely comments on his own constructive artifice. Graham Greene, the twentieth-century Roman Catholic novelist, speaks of Sterne's writing being like 'the daydream conversation of a man with a stutter in a world of his imagination'.

Sterne makes merry with the ills that flesh is heir to; the life of his 'small hero', Tristram, is one long chapter of accidents. His conception is flawed because his father is not concentrating at the time; his wife has suddenly asked him, 'Pray my dear, have you not forgot to wind up the clock?' This information comes to Tristram through his Uncle Toby, who reports that 'My Tristram's misfortunes began nine months before ever he came into the world.'

Tristram's father, Walter Shandy, is a retired merchant, in his mid-fifties. It has been his custom to wind up the clock on the first Sunday evening of every month and to make love to his wife at the same intervals. Mrs. Shandy thus associated the two affairs in her mind. Tristram's misfortunes come thick and fast. He complains that the world is vile:

> . . .—for I can truly say, that from the first hour I drew my breath in it, to this, that I can now scarce draw it at all, for an asthma I got in skating against the wind in *Flanders*;—I have been the continual sport of what the world calls Fortune [who] . . . has pelted me with a set of as pitiful misadventures and cross accidents as ever small HERO sustained.

The marriage settlement between Walter and his wife Elizabeth stipulated that any child born to them could be born, if Mrs. Shandy wished it, in London. But this agreement was to be annulled if Mrs. Shandy should imagine her labour had started when it had not in fact done so. However, as Mrs. Shandy had been to London the previous year, at a time inconvenient to her husband, he decided that her child must be born in the country after all. The result is that Tristram is delivered with forceps, and his nose is crushed flat. This is an indirect result of the obstetrician, Dr. Slop's, annoyance because Dr. Slop is a Roman Catholic and Uncle Toby, Walter's brother, whistles 'Lillabullero', a Protestant war-song.

Walter's response to family disaster, such as his son's mangled nose (and later the death of his elder son, Bobby), is to make long, rambling, learned disquisitions, for Walter has lost touch with his own instincts; he is a severed head. Uncle Toby, on the other hand, is all gentleness and emotion, although his hobby is re-enacting battles in miniature on a bowling green. Tristram's father wanted the boy named Trismegistus, after an ancient philosopher, but all the maid Susannah, responsible for rushing the child to a hasty baptism (for it was believed that if a child died unbaptised, instead of going to the Christian heaven it would languish forever in limbo), can remember is 'Tris—something' and the curate says the only Christian name in the world with such a beginning is 'Tristram'.

> Then 'tis *Tristram-gistus*, quoth *Susannah*.
> —There is no *gistus* to it, noodle! 'tis my own name, replied the curate, dipping his hand as he spoke into the bason—*Tristram!* said he &c. &c.

'Tristram', although a Celtic name meaning 'tumult', is also associated with French *tristesse* and the tragic tale of Tristram and Iseult.

When Tristram has reached the age of 5, lacking a chamberpot, Susannah persuades him to urinate out of a window, but the sash-cord breaks, the window falls and poor Tristram is accidentally circumcised. His father, instead of seeing to the boy's injury, goes off into a long account of the history of circumcision. When the news of brother Bobby's death is received, all Walter can do is spout from his learned reading. Susannah the maid thinks of the clothes she will inherit from her mistress's wardrobe, when Mrs. Shandy is in mourning, the fat scullion congratulates herself on still being alive. Only Corporal Trim, Uncle Toby's batman (officer's servant), responds with decent normal feeling:

> I lament for him from my heart and my soul, said *Trim*, fetching a sigh.—Poor creature!—poor boy! poor gentleman!. . . .
> 'Are we not here now;'—continued the corporal, 'and are we not'—(dropping his hat plumb upon the ground—and pausing, before he pronounced the word)—'gone! in a moment?' The descent of the hat was as if a heavy lump of clay had been kneaded into the crown of it.—Nothing could have expressed the sentiment of mortality, of which it was the type and fore-runner, like it,—his hand seemed to vanish from under it,—it fell dead,—the corporal's eye fix'd upon it, as upon a corps,—and *Susannah* burst into a flood of tears.

Volume VI relates the pathetic tale of Lieutenant Le Fever and his son, together with Toby's great kindness to them. Mr. and Mrs. Shandy decide it is time to put Tristram into breeches. The book also describes the military model of earthworks that Toby and Trim are building in the garden. The paradox is that Uncle Toby, the ex-soldier, is gentle as a lamb, unwilling to hurt a fly, assuring it that 'This world is surely wide enough to hold both thee and me.' The pursuit of Uncle Toby by the Widow Wadman is started. But in Volume VII the narrative thread, such as it is, is broken by a description of Tristram's travels in France (a fictionalized version of Sterne's own doomed search for health). In Volume VIII we return to the developing romance between Toby and the widow. Volume IX includes the story of poor Maria of Moulins, a girl who has been driven mad by a disappointment in love. She reappears in *A Sentimental Journey*. Maria is possibly an emblem of the grief-stricken artist, for she is a musician. She sits upon a bank playing on her pipe, with her little goat beside her.

> . . . she was in a thin white jacket with her hair, all but two tresses, drawn up into a silk net, with a few olive-leaves twisted a little fantastically on one side—she was beautiful; and if ever I felt the full force of an honest heart-ache, it was the moment I saw her—
> —God help her! Poor damsel! Above a hundred masses, said the postillion, have been said in the several parish churches and convents around, for her,—but without effect; we have still hopes, as she is sensible for short intervals, that the Virgin at last will restore her to herself; but her parents, who know her best, are hopeless upon that score, and think her senses are lost for ever.
> As the postillion spoke this, MARIA made a cadence so melancholy, so tender and querulous, that I sprung out of the chaise to help her, and found myself sitting betwixt her and her goat before I relapsed from my enthusiasm.
> MARIA look'd wistfully for some time at me, and then at her goat—and then at me—and then at her goat again, and so on, alternately—
> —Well, Maria, said I softly—What resemblance do you find?

Sterne's mixture of moods, in such passages as this, the mixture of tenderness and delicate humour, is original with him. Nineteenth-century commentators, upset by his love of bawdy double meanings, under-estimated the importance of his intellectual content. The philosopher John Locke, in his *Essay Concerning Human Understanding* (1690), had written:

> Wit lying in the assemblage of ideas, and putting those together with quickness and variety, wherein can be found any resemblance or congruity thereby to make up pleasant pictures in the fancy. Judgement, on the contrary, lies in separating carefully one from the other, ideas, wherein can be found the least difference, thereby to avoid being misled by similitude.

This passage was enormously influential, and Locke's definition of these terms changed the meaning of 'wit', which had previously included in its meanings 'intellect' as well as 'creative imagination', so that it became downgraded to something more frivolous, and inferior to 'judgement'.

The poet Alexander Pope, in his *Essay on Criticism* (1711), had resisted the tendency of Locke to separate wit and judgement with his epigram: 'For wit and judgement often are at strife,/ Though meant each other's aid, like man and wife.' Pope also wrote, in the same poem, '*True* Wit is *Nature* to Advantage drest,/ What oft was *Thought*, but ne'er so well *Exprest*.'

Dr. Samuel Johnson wrote that Pope had 'reduced wit from strength of thought to happiness of language', but Pope was not really to blame; the damage had already been done by Locke. Later, the Romantic poets were to re-emphasize the importance of the emotions, but Sterne was a pioneer. Sterne sets out to heal the split between wit and judgement, and makes a characteristically witty demonstration, using two knobs on the back of a chair:

> —Here stands *wit*,—and there stands *judgement*, close beside it, just like the two knobs I'm speaking of, upon the back of this self same chair on which I am sitting.
>
> You see, they are the highest and most ornamental parts of its *frame*,—as wit and judgement are of *ours*,—and like them too, indubitably both made and fitted to go together, in order as we say in all such cases of duplicated embellishments,—*to answer one another*. . . .
>
> Now these two knobs—or top ornaments of the mind of man, which crown the whole entablature,—being, as I said, wit and judgement, which of all others, as I have proved it, are the most needful,—the most priz'd,—the most calamitous to be without, and consequently the hardest to come at. . . .
>
> I need not tell your worships, that this was done with so much cunning and artifice,—that the great *Locke*, who was seldom outwitted by false sounds,—was nevertheless bubbled here. . . .
>
> This has been made the *Magna Charta* of stupidity ever since. . . .

To be 'bubbled' is to be fooled. Sterne, in his jocular, sceptical enquiry into the nature of existence, pleads for a balance between thought and feeling, using his practised skills as a preacher, an expositor of moral doctrines, in order to stimulate and amuse us, the readers. The late Dr. Leavis, of Cambridge, wrote of 'Sterne's irresponsible (and nasty) trifling'. Dr. Samuel Johnson wrote, 'Nothing odd will do. *Tristram Shandy* did not last.' Both the great doctors have been proved, I believe, wrong.

We recognize our own anxious, inconclusive selves, in search of healing and stability, when we read:

> Every line I write, I feel an abatement of the quickness of my pulse, and of that careless alacrity with it, which every day of my life prompts me to say and write a thousand things I should not.—And this moment that I last dipp'd my pen into my ink, I could not help taking notice what a cautious air of sad composure and solemnity there appear'd in my manner of doing it.—Lord! art wont, *Tristram!* to transact it with in other humours, . . .

Our century, in which psychotherapy is a boom industry, can hardly afford to mock Sterne's anxieties. For him, medicine was not an alien world of incomprehensible theories and dehumanizing scientific models of man. It provided him, as does the language of social psychology today, with a means and a language for trying to understand the human condition, which included, of course, his own, as we progress through what he called 'this fragment of life'.

Wilbur Cross, Sterne's biographer, notes that all of Sterne's digressions, which he called 'the sunshine of life and the soul of reading' start from some ludicrous incident or casual remark. Sterne's other work, *A Sentimental Journey Through France and Italy* (1768), is a fictionalized travel diary, based on Sterne's own travels between 1762 and 1765, and is believed to be the first English novel which survives in a handwritten manuscript. The book is only ambiguously a novel; it contemptuously parodies Tobias Smollett's sour and angry *Travels Through France and Italy* (1766). In Sterne's work Smollett appears as 'Smelfungus', whose irritability is in total contrast to the gentle charity with which Parson Yorick (an idealized portrait of a cleric taken over from *Tristram Shandy*) observes the life of foreign parts. Whereas Smollett grouses about the rapacity of the natives, Yorick sees only charming women, everywhere, and flirts discreetly with them. The book belongs to the tradition of the 'Sentimental novel' or 'Novel of sensibility'. Towards the end of *A Sentimental Journey*, Sterne writes:

> Dear sensibility! source inexhausted of all that's precious in our joys, or costly in our sorrows! thou chainest the martyr down upon his bed of straw—and 'tis thou who lifts him up to HEAVEN—eternal fountain of our feelings!—'tis here I trace thee—and this is thy divinity which stirs within me—not, that in some sad and sickening moments, *'my soul shrinks back upon herself, and startles at destruction'*—mere pomp of words!—but that I feel some generous joys and cares beyond myself—all comes from thee, great—great *SENSORIUM* of the world!

The 'sensorium' means the brain as the organ of mind and the centre of nervous energy; there is also present, perhaps, something of Pope's expression of pantheistic faith, in *An Essay on Man*, Book II: 'All are but parts of one stupendous whole,/ Whose body Nature is and God the soul.'

Sensibility was the bond of compassion which bound man to man, whatever science told contemporaries about a mechanistic universe. The object of the sentimental novel was to illustrate the combination of quivering sensitivity with strict virtue and honour. Precursors were Richardson, Sarah Fielding and Henry Brooke (*The Fool of Quality* (1765)). A later example was Henry Mackenzie's *The Man of Feeling*. Jane Austen's *Northanger Abbey* mocks the 'refined susceptibilities' of the Novel of Sentiment, and *Sense and Sensibility*, with a lingering backward glance, comes down on the side of common sense, though the victory is neither so unequivocal nor so complete as some commentators have supposed. Horace Walpole, four years younger than Sterne, said, 'This world is a comedy to those that think, a tragedy to those that feel.'

A Sentimental Journey, like *Tristram Shandy*, shows an oscillation between emotion and analytic commentary on it, and gives to Sterne his peculiar mood. Yorick as narrator observes himself with ironic detachment. Like Fielding before him, Sterne is concerned with works as well as faith, and is in line with the Latitudinarian divines who were anti-Puritan, anti-Stoic and anti-Hobbes. Thomas Hobbes was the seventeenth-century philosopher who said that man was ruled by self-interest alone and that only strong government held down his bad passions. Fielding and Sterne believed in practical charity or 'benevolence'. Partaking of the joys of life is to fulfil God's plan, in Sterne's view, a redemptive process. He writes:

> The learned *SMELFUNGUS* travelled from Boulogne to Paris—from Paris to Rome—and so on—but he set out with the spleen and jaundice, and every object he pass'd by was discoloured or distorted—He wrote an account of them, but 'twas nothing but the account of his miserable feelings. . . . Mundungus . . . made the whole tour . . . without one generous connection or pleasurable anecdote to tell of; but he had travell'd straight on looking neither to his right hand or his left, least Love or Pity should seduce him out of his road.
>
> Peace be to them! if it is to be found; but heaven itself, was it possible to get there with such tempers, would want objects to give it—every gentle spirit would come flying upon the wings of Love to hail their arrival—Nothing would the souls of Smelfungus and Mundungus hear of, but fresh anthems of joy, fresh raptures of love, and fresh congratulations of their common felicity—I heartily pity them: they have brought up no faculties for this work; and was the happiest mansion in heaven to be allotted to Smelfungus and Mundungus, they would be so far from being happy, that the souls of Smelfungus and Mundungus would do penance there to all eternity.

('Mundungus' was Samuel Sharp, who, like Smollett, was unenthusiastic about the beauties of Italy, but suggested a more efficient way of transporting dung into Naples.) *A Sentimental Journey* is written to 'teach us to love the world and our fellow-creatures'. Yorick travels with light-hearted irony as well as tender feelings.

The book opens, as it were, in mid-conversation: 'They order, said I, these matters better in France. . . .' Yorick travels from Calais through Rouen and Paris almost to Lyons, accompanied by his servant, La Fleur. He meets marquises and potboys, ladies of wealth and elegance, chambermaids and shopgirls, and he records his meeting with poor mad Maria.

Sterne asked in a sermon, 'For what purpose do you imagine, has God made us? for the social sweets of the well watered vallies where he has planted us, or for the dry and dismal deserts of a *Sierra Morena*?'

In *A Sentimental Journey*, he writes:

> I pity the man who can travel from *Dan* to *Beersheba*, and cry, 'Tis all barren—and so it is; and so is all the world to him who will not cultivate the fruits it offers. I declare, said I, clapping my hands chearily together, that was I in a desart, I would find out wherewith in it to call forth my affections.

Despite his own physical wretchedness, Sterne asserted that *Tristram Shandy* was 'writ . . . against the *SPLEEN*' or depression; in one of his sermons he said it was his 'conviction . . . that the principal spirit in the Universe is one of joy'.

4

Jane Austen: Quiet Satirist

Jane Austen was born on 16 December 1775. She died on 18 July 1817 and is buried in the north aisle of Winchester Cathedral. The most recent biography was published in 1987 by Park Honan, Professor of English and American Literature at the University of Leeds.

Jane Austen was author of six novels, all of which are still read and enjoyed. Her first book was *Sense and Sensibility* (1811), followed by her most popular and famous book, *Pride and Prejudice* (1813), *Mansfield Park* (1814), and *Emma* (1816). *Northanger Abbey* and *Persuasion* were published post-humously in 1818.

Jane was described by her nephew, J. E. Austen-Leigh, the youngest member of the family to attend her funeral, as very attractive. She had naturally curly brown hair, and bright hazel eyes, like those of her heroine, Emma Woodhouse. She had a clear complexion, with round pink cheeks and a small, neat nose and mouth. The only authenticated portrait of her is a sketch by her sister Cassandra, who was generally considered handsomer than Jane. Both women, neither of whom ever married, early adopted the custom of wearing caps, then the mark of the middle-aged, rather early in life. They were neatly, but not fashionably, dressed. They never had much money.

Fond of music, Jane had a sweet voice, both in singing and in conversation. She played the piano and practised every morning before breakfast, and in the evening she often accompanied herself as she sang old songs. She read French fluently and knew some Italian. She was fond of reading history and at 15 she wrote a 'History of England from the reign of

Henry the 4th to the death of Charles the 1st by a partial, prejudiced and ignorant historian'. Its prejudices are violently conservative: she defended Mary, Queen of Scots, against her cousin Elizabeth, admiring Mary for being constant to her religion (then a highly controversial opinion), and regarded Charles I as a martyr. In *Northanger Abbey* Jane makes her heroine's friend, Eleanor Tilney, a reader of history and biography. Eleanor is shown as very intelligent. Jane's dearest friend was her sister Cassandra, and most of Jane's surviving letters are to her. Unfortunately, after Jane died, Cassandra went through the letters and destroyed several she considered too private for posterity to see. Cassandra was engaged to a young clergyman, too poor to marry. The young couple were not too downcast, however, for the young man, Thomas Fowle, hoped to be given a living by Lord Craven, to whom he was distantly related and who was a personal friend. In the French wars, Thomas went with Lord Craven as chaplain to his regiment to the West Indies, but died of yellow fever at San Domingo. Lord Craven, stricken with remorse, later said that if he had known that poor Thomas was about to be married, he would never have allowed the young man to go with him to such an unhealthy place. Jane grew up aware that her sister's life had been blighted by this loss. The sisters were always close; when Cassandra went to boarding school, little Jane, three years younger, went with her. Their mother was heard to say, 'If Cassandra were going to have her head cut off, Jane would insist on sharing her fate!' The sisters shared a small bedroom all Jane's life, and most of her novels must have been written in the sitting room, where she could be interrupted at any time. Jane was secretive about her work, and wrote on small sheets of paper that could easily be hidden underneath pieces of blotting paper. There was a swing door that creaked when it was opened, and she would never allow the hinge to be oiled, because the creaking noise warned her that someone was coming and gave her a few precious minutes to conceal what she was up to. This door still exists in Jane Austen's last home at Chawton, Hampshire, and still creaks. The house is a museum and the state of the door is a mark of respect and a memorial curiosity.

From childhood, Jane scribbled stories, sketches, jokes, and wrote plays which her brothers and sisters performed for the amusement of their parents. Her early work shows an ability to see through stale conventional sentiment and style, and to mock current clichés. When she grew up, her playful and amusing talk was the delight of her nieces, to whom she showed great sweetness of manner and that serious attention which endears adults to children. She told them stories of fairyland, serials which could go on for days at a time. She also lent them her clothes for dressing up. After she died, the nieces found themselves thinking, 'I must keep this for Aunt Jane.' She inspired love, though her wit, in her letters and in her novels, could be acid.

Both sides of her family were distinguished for intelligence. Her maternal grandfather was a clergyman who had been a Fellow of All Souls, Oxford, and whose brother was Master of Balliol College, Oxford, for fifty odd years. Jane's father, George Austen, was an orphan, who owed his education to an uncle, a successful lawyer called Francis Austen. George Austen was exceptionally handsome, charming and clever. From Tonbridge School he won a scholarship to St. John's College, Oxford, and became a Fellow of his college. In 1764 he became rector of two parishes under the system of patronage then obtaining. One living, Deane, in Hampshire, was bought for him by his generous uncle Francis, and Steventon, next door to it, was given him by his cousin Mr. Knight. Steventon was Jane Austen's childhood home, which she left with regret on the death of her father. The combined population of the two parishes was about 300 people. Their father as a clergyman and Oxford graduate had status as an intellectual, but lacked the money to compete with the local landowners. Jane Austen writes about the gentry and the clergy. In general, the clergy were drawn from the younger sons of good families, who had education but small means.

Jane was one of eight children. Her eldest brother, James, became a clergyman like his father. There was a second brother, who was in some way handicapped, who died young. Two of Jane's brothers, Francis ('Frank') and Charles, who went into the navy at the age of 12 because there was no money to educate them or buy them commissions in the army, became Admirals. Jane followed their adventures round the world and followed their careers with passionate interest. Her admiration for the navy is demonstrated in *Mansfield Park* and in *Persuasion*. Although, as we learn from *Northanger Abbey*, it was considered incorrect for women to discuss politics in mixed company, her letters reflect a lively concern with current affairs. When she was a year old, Britain lost the American colonies in their War of Independence, an economic blow to Britain, for it meant the loss of trade worth £2,000,000 a year. Jane's cousin, Eliza Hancock, married a French count who lost his head on the guillotine in 1794. The widow, now the Countess de Feuillide, came back to England and married Jane's brother Henry, a failed banker who became a clergyman in middle age. Social and economic distress combined with radical ideas from across the Channel to threaten the privileged classes. The increasing wealth of the manufacturers was threatening the traditional hereditary leaders of society. Although it is frequently said that her novels show nothing of the upheavals around her (the French Revolution, the Napoleonic wars, unemployment, poverty and riots), they can be glimpsed in her pages as background to the humdrum lives of her characters, just as we receive images of distant wars on our television sets, but continue our lives undisturbed. And in *Pride and Prejudice* and *Emma* her material is the struggle for dominance between the well-born and the new rich.

Jane herself led a quiet life as the unmarried daughter of a widowed mother, living on the charity of her brothers. Edward, the third brother, had been adopted by the rich cousin, Mr. Knight, and inherited his estate. The family had connections and education, but were not rich, and Jane Austen's novels deal with the problems of young women who would like to marry but are hampered by their lack of dowries. She belonged to the upper bourgeoisie and, at that period, women of her class were not allowed by custom to work for wages. The only course open to a middle-class girl with no money who could not find a husband was to become a governess. In *Emma* Jane Fairfax, faced with this miserable prospect, compares the trade in governesses to 'the slave trade'. Governesses were exploited and isolated, not the social equals of the families who employed them, yet too well-educated to mix comfortably with the other servants. Ladies worked at home, to be sure. Most of the sewing was done by 'ladies', who made with their own hands all the shirts worn by their fathers and brothers, all the family linen (a word which meant shirts, underwear, bedsheets, towels and so on). In the museum at Chawton, there is still a patchwork quilt made up of small scraps of printed fabric, cut and sewn into a beautiful, complex pattern in blue, rust red, brown and cream-colour, made by Jane herself with her mother and Cassandra. Jane Austen was 'clever with her hands': she wrote in a letter, '. . . an artist cannot do anything slovenly' (to Cassandra, 17 November 1798). Her handwriting was clear and elegant. In her day, there were no envelopes: letters had to be folded. Some people's letters looked loose and untidy, but Jane's were folded with perfect neatness and the sealing wax dropped on to the correct spot.

Jane Austen wrote about the world and the people she knew, the quiet life of the country families from the late 1790s till 1815. She wrote to her niece Anna Austen, who also aspired to be a novelist,

> You are now collecting your People delightfully, getting them exactly into such a spot as is the delight of my life; 3 or 4 Families in a Country Village is the very thing to work on. . . . [9 September 1814]

Jane advised her niece against moving the story to Ireland, where 'the manners might be different'. In a letter to her nephew Edward, the author of the *Memoir*, she compared herself to a miniaturist, using a 'little bit (two inches wide) of Ivory on which I work with so fine a Brush' and which 'produces little effect after much labour' (to J. E. Austen-Leigh, 16 December 1816).

She may have been mock-modest here, as she was in her correspondence with the Prince Regent's librarian, a Mr. Clarke, who wrote inviting her to dedicate her next work to the Prince. Mr. Clarke, a clergyman, took it upon himself to suggest a subject. Jane's next book should be about 'a clergyman, who should pass his time between the metropolis and the country'.

Tactfully, Jane replied that she was honoured. In a letter dated 11 December 1815, she said:

> The comic part of the character I might be equal to, but not the good, the enthusiastic, the literary. Such a man's conversation must at times be on subjects of science and philosophy, of which I know nothing; or at least be occasionally abundant in quotations and allusions which a woman who, like me, knows only her own mother tongue, and has read very little in that, would be totally without the power of giving. A classical education or at any rate a very extensive acquaintance with English literature, ancient and modern, appears to me quite indispensable for the person who would do justice to your clergyman; and I think I may boast myself to be, with all possible vanity, the most unlearned and uninformed female who ever dared to be an authoress.

Jane was unduly modest about her literary culture. However, she found herself in a trap common among novelists: she was pestered by somebody who wanted her to write up his ideas instead of her own. Mr. Clarke persisted, refusing to take the hint. Perhaps, he suggested, Jane might like to write 'an historical romance illustrative of the august house of Coburg. . .'.

Jane replied politely:

> . . . I am fully sensible that an historical romance founded on the house of Saxe Coburg, might be much more to the purpose of profit and popularity than such pictures of domestic life in country villages as I deal in. But I could no more write a romance than an epic poem. I could not seriously sit down to write a serious romance under any other motive than to save my life; and if it were indispensable for me to keep it up and never relax into laughing at myself or at other people, I am sure I should be hung before I had finished the first chapter. No, I must keep to my own style and go on in my own way. . . .

This was official correspondence. In her letters to her sister Cassandra she was less inhibited, allowing herself more sarcasm and less exasperated modesty.

She writes of *Pride and Prejudice* (14 February 1813):

. . . I am quite vain enough, and well satisfied enough. The work is rather too light, and bright, and sparkling; it wants shade; it wants to be stretched out here and there with a long chapter of sense, if it could be had; if not, of solemn specious nonsense, about something unconnected with the story; an essay on writing, a critique on Walter Scott, or the history of Buonaparte.

Sir Walter Scott was the famous poet against whose success the young writer was unwillingly forced to measure her own. Jealously, she joked, Walter Scott had no business to write novels because 'he has Fame and Profit enough as a Poet, and should not be taking the bread out of other people's mouths.—I do not like him, and do not mean to like *Waverley*' (to Anna Austen, 28 September 1814).

Scott wrote in his diary, 14 March 1826:

Read again, for the third time at least, Miss Austen's finely written novel of 'Pride and Prejudice'. The young lady had a talent for describing the involvements and feelings and characters of ordinary life, which is to me the most wonderful I ever met with. The big Bow Wow strain I can do myself like any now going; but the exquisite touch which renders ordinary commonplace things and characters interesting from the truth of the description and the sentiment is denied to me. What a pity such a gifted creature died so early!

Jane Austen's skill as a miniaturist has always been acknowledged. During the twentieth century, her reputation has risen steadily, as the view that she was complacent about a trivial society has given way to the view that she savagely satirizes it. But the charge that she did not respond to, nor reflect, the events of her day has echoed from the Prince Regent's librarian down to the present day. Yet she reflects social and economic change, and her wit and satire take as their material the responses of her characters to these changes. She has often been accused of snobbery. Readers have been misled by her use of words like 'breeding' and 'decorum', which in her day meant merely politeness or good manners. Other readers dislike the indubitably conservative tendency of her books, though better understood she may be seen as a conservationist rather than as a die-hard reactionary.

She satirizes the complacency of the self-satisfied people

she lived among, and the mindless triviality of their pursuits. Tied in with the class-war between old breeding and new money is the question of marriage. Jane Austen wrote about the tensions between love and money because this was the most acute problem for women of her class in her day. With no power of earning, the choice of a husband becomes more than a matter of pleasing oneself. Jane Austen's characters are told it is their duty to marry, if necessary against their own inclinations, to relieve their relatives of the burden of keeping them. A contemporary, Mrs. Jane West, wrote, 'The market is full of well-dressed spinsters.' Economic security was not easily obtained: the legitimate object of marriage was to acquire it, combined with emotional security. All Jane Austen's heroines manage it, though none of them finds it easy. She writes about the temptation to make a marriage of convenience, without love. In real life, many women did so because they had no choice. Jane did become engaged to a man six years younger than herself, but changed her mind next morning.

Jane jokes about the desperate last-chance marriage of an acquaintance, who had in middle age accepted a Mr. Wake:

> Maria, good-humoured and handsome and tall,
> For a husband was at her last stake;
> And having in vain danced at many a ball,
> Is now happy to jump at a Wake.

The neat pun is twofold: Maria 'jumps' now, a hasty and undignified action in pursuit of a husband, compared with dancing; in Ireland a 'wake' is the gathering that precedes a funeral. The flippant verse has a sad undersong. Jane wrote about the plight of bourgeois women, trapped in their social circumstances, recognizing the falsity of their lives, but with no opportunity to change them. The only weapon Jane's heroines have is their intelligence, combined with moral principle and a sense of humour.

Each of Jane Austen's heroines has to grow up, develop, learn to understand herself and other people, compromise with society yet keep her integrity.

Northanger Abbey was sold to a publisher in 1803, but publication was delayed until after the author's death, when it appeared together with *Persuasion*. Catherine Morland, a country clergyman's daughter, is taken to Bath for the season by her friends, Mr. and Mrs. Allen. At a dance she meets the Rev. Henry Tilney and his sister Eleanor. Catherine is unsophisticated, and the kindly Tilneys take her education in hand. Catherine also meets the feather-brained Isabella Thorpe, who is engaged to Catherine's brother James, and her awful lout of a brother, John Thorpe. Henry's father, General Tilney, has heard gossip that Catherine is an heiress, so she is invited to Northanger Abbey, the Tilneys' medieval country seat. Catherine and Isabella share a passion for the Gothic tales of Mrs. Radcliffe, and enjoy scaring themselves about skeletons and black veils. Catherine becomes convinced that the General must have murdered his wife and is humiliated when Henry discovers her fantasy. It is John Thorpe who has originally led General Tilney to believe Catherine is rich; now he exaggerates her poverty, and the General sends Catherine packing. Henry remains loyal to Catherine and asks her to marry him. Eleanor meanwhile has made a good marriage, and the General has discovered that Catherine's family are not, after all, beggars. Henry and Catherine are married, with the General's consent.

Sense and Sensibility was published first of Jane Austen's novels, in 1811. The widowed Mrs. Dashwood has three daughters, Elinor, Marianne and Margaret. They are short of money, because John Dashwood, son of the first wife, has disobeyed his father's injunction to take care of his stepmother and half-sisters. John has a greedy wife, formerly a Miss Ferrars. However, Edward Ferrars, Mrs. John Dashwood's brother, is attracted to Elinor Dashwood and she to him, but Edward seems strangely unwilling to commit himself. The Dashwoods move to a cottage in Devonshire, where living is cheaper. There Marianne meets the fascinating John Willoughby, and falls wildly in love with him, expecting marriage. But Willoughby disappears to London and when Marianne approaches him, he rebuffs her and tells her he is to marry a rich woman. Marianne collapses. Elinor has her own troubles: she learns from the unpleasant Lucy Steele that Edward Ferrars is secretly engaged to Lucy. This has been kept secret, because Edward is financially depend- ent on his mother. Mrs. Ferrars does find out and tries to wean Edward away from Lucy, but he is too honourable to break the tie he now regrets (at the time a man could not honourably break an engagement: the woman had to 'release' him from it). In her baffled fury, Mrs. Ferrars gives to Edward's younger brother, Robert, the property which is Edward's by right. Robert, however, falls in love with Lucy, who, having an eye to the main chance and preferring the richer man, elopes with him, leaving Edward free to marry Elinor. He becomes a clergyman and gets a living. 19-year-old Marianne, on the rebound, marries the good, kind, worthy Colonel Brandon, 31 years old, who wears flannel waist- coats.

Pride and Prejudice (1813) was rejected in its first draft.

Like the Dashwood girls, the Bennet girls have more taste and charm than money. Mr. and Mrs. Bennet have five daughters, but the property is entailed to a cousin, the Rev. William Collins, who is the protegé of the arrogant Lady Catherine de Bourgh. Charles Bingley rents Netherfield near where the Bennet girls live, and he and the eldest, Jane, fall in love. Bingley is a friend of Lady Catherine's nephew, Fitzwilliam Darcy, who is unwillingly attracted to the witty second daughter, Elizabeth. But Elizabeth dislikes his *hauteur* and believes George Wickham, son of Darcy's steward, when he complains of Darcy's behaviour. Darcy and Bingley's snobbish sisters persuade Bingley to leave the district and Jane.

Meanwhile, the complacent and thick-witted Mr. Collins feels it his duty to marry one of the girls, to mitigate the injustice of the entail. Hearing that Jane is likely to become engaged, he proposes to Elizabeth. When she refuses, he asks her friend Charlotte Lucas, who accepts at once. Elizabeth visits the couple and runs into Darcy, who is visiting Lady Catherine. Darcy proposes marriage, letting her know plainly he does not think her family good enough for him. Elizabeth, furious, rejects him. Darcy writes to Elizabeth exposing Wick- ham's failings and explaining that he separated Bingley from Jane because he did not believe she cared.

Elizabeth travels north with her pleasant uncle and aunt,

Mr. and Mrs. Gardiner, and calls in at Pemberley, Darcy's house. To Elizabeth's embarrassment, he comes home earlier than expected. When Elizabeth hears that her foolish youngest sister Lydia has run away with Wickham, Darcy helps bring about the marriage which alone can save Lydia's honour. Bingley and Jane become engaged and, despite squawks of protest from Lady Catherine, so do Darcy and Elizabeth. Jane Austen's favourite heroine was Elizabeth Bennet. In an exhibition of portraits, she reported that she found a tolerable likeness of Mrs. Bingley, but could find no picture that answered her idea of Mrs. Darcy.

Mansfield Park was published in 1814.

Sir Thomas Bertram of Mansfield Park has two sons, the wastrel Tom and the conscientious Edmund, and two daughters, Maria and Julia. He married the prettiest of three sisters. Sir Thomas kindly takes in his wife's niece, little Fanny Price, whose parents are struggling. Fanny is not the social equal of her cousins and suffers loneliness, softened by Edmund's friendship. Fanny falls in love with Edmund, and is grieved when he falls for the fascinating Mary Crawford, whose brother Henry selfishly plays havoc with the affections of Maria and Julia. Maria is about to make a worldly match with the rich but stupid Mr. Rushworth. After the marriage, Henry decides to 'make a little hole in Fanny Price's heart' and proposes. Fanny, knowing his real character, refuses, and is severely reprimanded by Sir Thomas for her ingratitude. Fanny is sent home to Portsmouth, which she comes to realize she has romanticized; she begins to appreciate the value of Mansfield. Henry runs away with Maria Rushworth and Julia runs away with the superficial Mr. Yates. When Mary Crawford shows she considers adultery not criminal but foolish, Edmund is disillusioned. He has had ample warning in her sneers at the clergy, which she has made knowing that Edmund is to be ordained. Edmund marries Fanny.

Emma was published in 1816. It is about the spoilt and self-satisfied lady of the manor who thinks she can organize other people's lives. Emma chooses to patronize Harriet Smith, a 17-year-old of unknown parentage, and decides that Harriet should marry the Vicar, Mr. Elton. Emma persuades Harriet to refuse the excellent Robert Martin, a respectable farmer.

This annoys Emma's brother-in-law's brother, Mr. George Knightley. Mr. Elton hovers round Emma and Harriet and Emma thinks her plan is working, until the hideous embarrassment of Mr. Elton's proposal to her, Emma. Mr. Elton is offended by her refusal and insulted by her suggestion that he should be addressing Miss Smith. He intends to do better than to marry a mere Miss Smith and shortly afterwards triumphantly produces a wife, not so rich as Emma (for Emma has £30,000), but with nearly £10,000. A young man called Frank Churchill, adopted by rich relatives, has finally come to visit his father, and flirts with Emma. But he is secretly engaged to Jane Fairfax, niece to Emma's impoverished neighbour, Miss Bates. Emma, ignorant of this attachment, encourages Harriet to hope for Frank, but Harriet, misunderstanding, prepares to fix her volatile affections on Mr. Knightley. Miss Bates is garrulous but good-hearted and bears her poverty cheerfully. Emma is rude to her in a careless moment and is severely reprimanded by Mr. Knightley for it. Eventually Emma marries Mr. Knightley and Harriet marries Robert Martin.

Persuasion was published after Jane Austen's death, together with *Northanger Abbey*, in 1818.

Sir Walter Elliot is a foolish, spendthrift baronet, vain of his looks and obsessed with his own importance. Running short of money, he has to rent out his house, Kellynch Hall. The eldest daughter Elizabeth is single at nearly 30. Anne, the heroine, is 27, having been persuaded to relinquish her romance with a young naval officer, Captain Frederick Wentworth. Wentworth is furious over the breach, Anne heartbroken. The tenant of Kellynch is Admiral Croft, who is married to Wentworth's sister, so Anne and Frederick meet again. The youngest Elliot daughter, Mary, a peevish moaner, is married to Charles Musgrove. Charles has two pretty sisters, Henrietta and Louisa, and Wentworth is attracted to Louisa, though his heart steals back towards Anne. Louisa is injured in an accident and during convalescence becomes engaged to another naval officer. Meanwhile, the Elliot family are living in Bath, where Anne meets a smooth and charming, but devious, cousin, a Mr. William Elliot, who is also scheming to get rid of a Mrs. Clay who

has designs on Sir Walter. Wentworth discovers by chance
that Anne still loves him, and they are married. Jane Austen
wrote to her niece Fanny Knight: 'You may *perhaps* like the
heroine, as she is almost too good for me.'

Jane Austen's most widely-known and best loved book
is *Pride and Prejudice*. It opens with a characteristically subtle
joke, which lays bare the anxieties of her social milieu:

> It is a truth universally acknowledged, that a single man
> in possession of a good fortune must be in want of a wife.
> However, little known the feelings or views of such a man
> may be on first entering a neighbourhood, this truth is so
> well fixed in the minds of the surrounding families, that he
> is considered as the rightful property of some one or other of
> their daughters.

The use of the word 'universally' is highly ironic: being translated, it means 'in provincial bourgeois society it is believed
that. . .'. Such obsession is far from universal. In other
words, the mothers and daughters in Jane Austen's society
want, need, rich men to be in search of wives, although it
is by no means certain that rich men are necessarily at all
interested in female company. The wish, says Jane Austen
slyly, by implication rather than direct statement, is father to
the thought. In the period men and women led separate lives.
The men spent their days in sport or politics, the women in
domesticity and visits. Beneath the balanced sentences we
have to supply our own knowledge of the manoeuvring to
ensnare a husband 'in possession of a good fortune'; we
recognize what we are to see in the novel, the undignified
scrambling among the local girls and their mothers to attract
the newcomer's attention.

The position of Elizabeth Bennet, the heroine of *Pride and
Prejudice*, is socially privileged but insecure. She speaks for
her generation when she asks, '. . . what is the difference,
in matrimonial affairs, between a mercenary and a prudent
motive? Where does discretion end, and avarice begin?' Her
father is a gentleman with a small estate. But the law of
inheritance means that it cannot go to his five daughters.
It has to go to a male heir, Mr. Bennet's cousin Mr. Collins.
In addition, Mr. Bennet has married a pretty, but foolish,
woman of a lower social class than his own. She soon bores

and irritates him so that he withdraws into idleness and sarcasm. Mrs. Bennet's anxiety to 'get her daughters married'
is laughable—or is it? Her plight is one of necessity. Mrs.
Bennet's 'solace was visiting and news'.

Elizabeth is the second daughter, not so beautiful as the
eldest sister, Jane. Mr. Bennet's property was

> an estate of two thousand a year . . . entailed on a distant rela-
> tion. Their mother's fortune, though ample for her situation in
> life, could but ill supply the deficiency of his. Her father had
> been an attorney in Meryton, and had left her four thousand
> pounds.

Entails held estates together. By the legal process of entail
the succession to an estate could be controlled for generations. The heir could not sell or mortgage except by Act
of Parliament, an expensive process. Wives usually brought
dowries or 'portions' with them, used to buy more land. The
entail, which Mrs. Bennet resents without understanding, is
responsible for the dilemma of the Bennet girls. As their
mother is bitterly aware, Mr. Collins, after Mr. Bennet dies,
will have the right, in Mr. Bennet's words, to 'turn you all
out of this house as soon as he pleases'. No wonder Mrs.
Bennet complains, 'I am sure I do not know who is to
maintain you when your father is dead.' No wonder she
has daydreams of a 'smart young colonel with five or six
thousand a year'.

Her daughters are handicapped socially as well as financially. Mrs. Hurst, sister of the eligible Mr. Bingley who has
come into the neighbourhood as a single man in possession
of a good fortune, says Jane Bennet, the eldest sister, is a very
sweet girl, 'but with such a father and mother, and such low
connections . . .' she will not quite do. It is mentioned that
their uncle is an attorney, an inferior sort of lawyer; another
'lives somewhere near Cheapside'. People of fashion did not
live near Cheapside, the commercial eastern part of London,
within the city. Mr. Bingley, who is not snobbish like his
sisters, says that these social disadvantages do not make
the girls any less agreeable, but the aristocratic Mr. Darcy
agrees with Mrs. Hurst and Miss Bingley that their low-class
relatives must damage the girls' prospects of marrying well.

Yet Jane Austen is at pains to show this judgement to be wrong. Elizabeth's uncle Mr. Gardiner, who is in business in London, is 'a sensible, gentlemanlike man' (high praise); his wife is 'an amiable, intelligent, elegant woman'. Mr. Darcy comes to recognize their worth. Jane Austen sharply criticizes the snobbery of Mr. Bingley's sisters. They 'would have had difficulty in believing that a man who lived by trade, and in view of his own warehouses, could have been so well-bred and agreeable'.

At the time, the gentry owned land and lived from rents and the sale of timber. The manufacturers struggled to make fortunes in trade so they could buy estates and, if they did not become respectable, their children stood a chance of doing so. Yet the Bingley fortune has been made in trade. The sisters are

> proud and conceited . . . had a fortune of twenty thousand pounds. . . . they were of a respectable family in the north of England, a circumstance more deeply impressed on their memories than that their brother's fortune and their own had been acquired in trade.

Mr. Bingley's income of £5,000 a year comes from the £100,000 left by his father who had intended to purchase the estate, but did not live to do it. Sometimes Bingley thinks he might settle at Netherfield, which he is renting, and leave the next generation to buy, but his sisters are 'very anxious for his having an estate of his own'. Mrs. Hurst, whose husband has style, but not too much money, likes to impose on her good-natured brother's hospitality. Elizabeth recognizes that Mr. Bingley's sisters look down on her family: 'We are not rich enough, or grand enough for them.' Despite Jane's beauty and Elizabeth's wit, the Bennet girls are not eligible. They have nothing to tempt suitors with. When Elizabeth asks her father to restrain Lydia's wildness lest she be taken advantage of, her father replies that Lydia is 'luckily too poor to be an object of prey to anybody'.

Mr. Collins clumsily tries to make up for the injustice by offering to marry one of the girls, who can then share the estate with him. Hearing that Jane is likely to become engaged, he proposes to Elizabeth, blandly unaware that his terms are insulting to her.

> To fortune I am perfectly indifferent, and shall make no demand of that nature on your father, since I am perfectly well aware that it could not be complied with; and that one thousand pounds in the four per cents which will not be yours till after your mother's decease is all that you may ever be entitled to. . . .

Mr. Collins is not unusual in making these calculations; he is merely tactless in mentioning them so bluntly to Elizabeth. When she refuses him, he tries to bring pressure on her by pointing out the brutal realities: 'Your portion is unhappily so small that it will in all likelihood undo the effects of all your loveliness and amiable qualifications.'

Mr. Collins is telling Elizabeth that a girl so poor as herself is unlikely to get another chance of marrying. Elizabeth, to her mother's annoyance, refuses Mr. Collins, but she knows the economic facts of life. 'Handsome young men must have something to live on, as well as the plain,' she says when the attractive adventurer Wickham deserts her to run after an heiress. When Wickham, whose plan has failed, runs away with Elizabeth's youngest sister Lydia, and it becomes urgent for them to marry in order to save Lydia's reputation, Elizabeth says sadly, 'Wickham will never marry a woman without some money. He cannot afford it.'

Mr. Bennet lets Lydia have £50 a year, the income on her inheritance of £1,000. Darcy's cousin Fitzwilliam, the younger son of an earl, spells out to Elizabeth that he cannot afford to be seriously interested in her. She says, recognizing this, 'Younger sons cannot marry where they like. Unless where they like women of fortune, which I think they very often do.' The young man replies, 'Our habits of expense make us too dependent, and there are not many in my rank of life who can afford to marry without some attention to money.' Miss Georgiana Darcy's fortune is £30,000, which explains why Wickham, the son of her father's steward, tried to run away with her. Until the Married Women's Property Act of 1870 a woman's property became her husband's unless a separate 'settlement' was made upon her. Each of Jane Austen's characters carries his or her price-tag—and

Elizabeth's is low. No wonder Lady Catherine de Bourgh, who wants Darcy for her own daughter, despises Elizabeth as a 'young woman without family, connections or fortune'. Elizabeth's engagement to Darcy is 'upstart pretension' and from Lady Catherine's point of view, that of the great world, so it is. For Elizabeth to catch Darcy, with his £10,000 a year, is indeed an amazingly good match, beyond any reasonable expectations. *Pride and Prejudice* is a Cinderella story. In the real world, people have to compromise, like Charlotte Lucas, who catches Mr. Collins after Elizabeth has rejected him. Charlotte marries 'solely from the pure and disinterested desire of an establishment'. Pure? Disinterested? Charlotte is marrying without love, in order to grab at a home of her own. Elizabeth tactlessly reveals her astonishment at the news of the engagement, Charlotte says quietly, 'I am not romantic, you know. I never was. I ask only a comfortable home.' The glittering prizes are few and far between; most people have to settle for what they can get.

> Mr. Collins . . . was neither sensible nor agreeable; his society was irksome . . . but still he would be her husband. Without thinking highly either of men or of matrimony, marriage had always been her object; it was the only honourable provision for well educated young women of small fortune, and however uncertain of giving happiness, must be their pleasantest preservative from want.

Charlotte knows such an opportunity does not come every day. She is, after all, 27. Charlotte is no fool and she makes the best of things. Charlotte sees shrewdly that Jane Bennet might not be successful in getting Bingley to marry her, though Jane loves Bingley very much. Jane keeps her feelings under such control that Darcy believes her to be indifferent, and causes Jane much heartache by persuading Bingley to move away. Charlotte observes: 'It is sometimes a disadvantage to be so very guarded. If a woman conceals her affection . . . from the object of it, she may lose the opportunity of fixing him.'

Pride and Prejudice is a comedy of money as much as of manners.

Jane Austen's earliest completed novel was *Northanger*

Abbey, which mocks the romantic thrillers of Jane Austen's day. The heroine, Catherine Morland, expects life to be like fiction. Yet in it Jane Austen defends fiction as a craft:

> If the heroine of one novel be not patronised by the heroine of another, from whom can she expect protection and regard. . . . Let us not desert one another; we are an injured body. Although our productions have afforded more extensive and unaffected pleasure than those of any other literary corporation in the world, no species of composition has been so much decried. . . . 'Oh! it is only a novel,' replies the young lady . . . only some work in which the greatest powers of the mind are displayed, in which the most thorough knowledge of human nature, the happiest delineation of its varieties, the liveliest effusions of wit and humour are conveyed to the world in the best chosen language.

We are not to take Jane Austen literally when she writes, 'A woman especially, if she have the misfortune of knowing anything, should conceal it as well as she can.' In the novel she exposes the brainless fatuity of Isabella Thorpe, who thinks only of clothes and men, and is out to marry money, despite pretending otherwise.

Sense and Sensibility is about two sisters, who are also impoverished. Marianne is wildly romantic, Elinor more sober and self-controlled. Marianne falls helplessly in love with a charming deceiver, Willoughby, and has a breakdown when he deserts her. Elinor has her own troubles, for the man she loves, Edward Ferrars, has become entangled with Lucy Steele, whose manners are as bad as her grammar. The novel makes it clear that Marianne, with 'a sense of honour so keen, a generosity so romantic', is nevertheless selfish in indulging her feelings. Elinor's 'feelings were strong; but she knew how to control them'. Elinor suffers in silence, out of consideration for others. Marianne, repentant after her illness, admits to 'fretful selfishness'. Elinor, in her rational self-control, is wiser and more admirable than Marianne, although she seems less attractive to us. Yet there is a suppressed feminist plea embedded in the novel. Marianne, disappointed in Willoughby, who has married for money, turns to Colonel Brandon, who is almost twice her age, and marries him, and we are told that eventually she fell in love

with him. But it is stated earlier that Marianne marries partly
to please her mother and Elinor.

> With such a confederacy against her—with a knowledge
> so intimate of his goodness—with a conviction of his fond
> attachment to herself, which at last, though long after it was
> observable to everybody else—burst on her—what could she do?

Just how are we to take the news that Marianne gives
her hand with 'no sentiment superior to strong esteem and
lively friendship' to a man who she has previously objected
to because he wears, like an elderly gentleman, a flannel
waistcoat?

Mansfield Park is another Cinderella story. The heroine,
Fanny, is an underprivileged child adopted by a rich aunt
and uncle (as Jane Austen's own brother was). Fanny is
treated as a social inferior to her cousins, but her rôle is to
show up their moral inferiority. Mansfield Park is disrupted
by a pair of newcomers, Mary and Henry Crawford. Fanny
is in love with her cousin Edmund, and watches with pain
when Edmund falls in love with the mercenary Mary. The
Crawfords are pleasant, well-informed and amusing conver-
sationalists. Yet they give themselves away with everything
they say, showing themselves to be hard, frivolous and
self-centred. Edmund, as the younger son, is going to be a
parish priest. This is not good enough for Mary, who mocks
religion and urges him to take up something smarter. During
a period of financial anxiety, while Sir Thomas Bertram is
away seeing to his West Indian estates, the young people
decide to act a play, *Lovers' Vows*. This was a popular play,
but Jane Austen and others considered it immoral, as it
showed the upper classes as decadent and the peasants as
noble, and the heroine, Agatha, is an unmarried mother. Sir
Thomas's elder daughter, Maria, is engaged to the rich but
stupid Mr. Rushworth. She would like to marry the attractive
Henry Crawford, but while the play is in rehearsal Henry
cruelly plays with the affections of both Maria and her sister
Julia, without committing himself. Sir Thomas comes home
and puts a stop to the play-acting, harmful, because of the
expense involved and because of the destabilizing effect on
relationships. Henry Crawford proposes to Fanny, who is

under pressure to accept him. Sir Thomas tells Fanny she is ungrateful. Fanny cannot tell Sir Thomas what havoc Henry has wrought to the emotional lives of her cousins, Maria and Julia. Sir Thomas, to teach Fanny a lesson, sends her home on a visit to her parents, which makes Fanny realize that Mansfield is more comfortable and civilized than the squalid house of a half-pay marine officer who swears. But Mansfield is morally corrupt. Maria, unable to get Henry, marries Mr. Rushworth, but elopes with Henry soon afterwards. Mary comments coolly on the 'folly' of the couple, whereas Fanny and Edmund are shocked at the wickedness of adultery. Edmund sees Fanny's worth and finally marries her. Sir Thomas realizes the education he gave his daughters was inadequate:

> He feared that principle, active principle, had been wanting, that they had never been properly taught to govern their inclinations and tempers, by that sense of duty which can alone suffice. They had been instructed theoretically in their religion, but never required to bring it into daily practice. To be distinguished for elegance and accomplishments—the authorised object of their youth—could have had no useful influence that way, no moral effect on the mind. He had meant them to be good, but his cares had been directed to the understanding and manners, not the disposition; and of the necessity of self-denial and humility, he feared they had never heard from any lips that could profit them.

The novel is also remarkable for its portrait of the managing, bullying, Aunt Norris, widow of a clergyman, who is a parasite on the Mansfield family, and her sister Lady Bertram, who spends her days on the sofa with her pug dog, making endless yards of fringe, and thinking of herself as very busy.

In *Emma*, the heroine's vision is bounded by a narrow and exclusive snobbery, which is corrected by experience. Emma is 'handsome, clever and rich' and imagines she knows what is best for everybody. She learns the truth through a series of mistakes painful for her and for those she meddles with. She objects to the young farmer, Robert Martin, as a husband for her friend Harriet Smith, because Emma could not possibly meet him socially. Emma, who has £30,000, assumes that Mr. Martin 'will be a completely gross, vulgar farmer—totally inattentive to appearances and thinking of nothing but profit and loss'. Emma imagines that her friendship can raise Harriet in the social scale, but this is wilful. Emma is rich and Harriet has nothing. Old money was better than new, but it was money that counted. Those who had once had some, but had sunk in the world, like Mrs. and Miss Bates, widow and daughter of a clergyman, were dependent on more affluent friends.

Mr. Knightley is rightly angry with Emma for making Harriet refuse Robert: 'A degradation to illegitimacy and ignorance to be married to a respectable, intelligent, gentleman-farmer!' We know Robert is to be respected, from the sensible letter he writes to Harriet proposing marriage. As Mr. Knightley says, Robert 'always speaks to the purpose; open, straightforward, and very well-judging'. These qualities are to be rated as more important than the deficiencies Emma finds in him, his 'awkward look and abrupt manner' and 'a voice . . . wholly unmodulated'. Character, in Jane Austen's books, is always more important than surface polish. Robert is a tenant, not a landowner, but he is not poor. Harriet reports that the Martins live very comfortably, with no indoors man-servant, but otherwise they want for nothing. Mrs. Martin, she says, has an upper maid who has lived twenty-five years with her. The testimony of faithful servants is always, in Jane Austen's work, a valuable clue to character.

We see Emma making a last-ditch stand against the new wealth rising all around her. Her attempt at exclusiveness is handled ironically and shown to be doomed. Emma likes to think of herself as dominant in the village of Highbury. She is not pleased to hear that the Coles are giving a dinner party. They are friendly folk, but they are of 'low origin, in trade, and only moderately genteel'. Formerly they had lived quietly, but now they were getting richer, had extended their house, taken on more servants, and were now nearly as rich as Emma herself. The Coles had started inviting people to dinner. Emma is sure they will not presume to ask her, nor Mr. Knightley, nor the Westons. 'Nothing should tempt her to go, if they did.' She wishes her father were not known to be a hypochondriac who never went out; if she refused an invitation, it would be put down to his worries about his health, and not recognized as a social snub.

> The Coles were very respectable in their way, but they ought
> to be taught that it was not for them to arrange the terms on
> which the superior families would visit them.

In the upshot, Mr. Knightley and the Westons are invited
by the Coles, and Emma is put out because they do not invite
her. When the invitation does come, she accepts it, and is
surprised to find she enjoys herself. It is her snobbery which
is the object of satire here. She is, of course, better educated
than people like the Coles. Mrs. Cole, the new rich lady, has a
grand piano which she cannot play. She kindly invites Emma
to use it. Jane Austen's socio-economic comedy deserves
analysis. Emma, hoping for the support of Mr. Knightley
and Mr. Weston in her snobbish exclusiveness, imagines she
is keeping up standards. Mr. Weston, who has married Miss
Taylor, Emma's governess, is not very different from the
Coles. He was 'born of a respectable family, which for the last
two or three generations had been rising into gentility and
property'. After marrying into the high and mighty Churchill
family and being left a widower, he leaves his captaincy in
the army and 'engaged in trade, having brothers already
established in a good way in London, which afforded him a
favourable opening'. Eventually Mr. Weston manages to buy
'a little estate . . . which he had always longed for—enough
to marry a woman as portionless as Miss Taylor'.

When Emma says to Mr. Weston's son, adopted by his
grand relatives and called Frank Churchill, that Jane Fairfax,
niece to Miss Bates, is doomed to be a governess, Mrs.
Weston says in gentle reproof, 'You get upon delicate subjects, Emma. Remember that I am here.' Normally Emma is a
stickler for social distinctions: she considers Frank Churchill's
'indifference to a confusion of rank bordered too much on
inelegance of mind'. The weight we are to attach to the
concept of 'inelegance' here is problematical, and calls in
question all Emma's values. But because Emma loves her
ex-governess, she does not classify her socially in the cool
way she does other people. Emma wants it both ways: she
wants class distinction to be preserved, but imagines she can
raise her friends by her notice.

When Mrs. Elton, the vicar's wife, whose snobbery and
pretensions parody and challenge Emma's own, is surprised

to find Mrs. Weston 'so very lady-like . . . quite the gentle-woman', Emma is furious. Miss Taylor has brought Emma up, so she must be acceptable. Mrs. Elton takes the cool social view of Mrs. Weston as the humble governess, the girl with no money who has snared a husband with property.

Friction arising from social pretensions and attempts at exclusiveness in a changing society is the staple of comedy in *Emma*. Mr. Weston complains of his first mother-in-law, Mrs. Churchill, that although she had no family herself, ever since she was 'turned into a Churchill' she had 'out-Churchill'd them all in high and mighty claims'. In herself, however, she was 'an upstart'.

Mrs. Elton responds, shuddering, with an account of some 'upstarts' called Tupman, near Maple Grove, where her sister and brother-in-law live. These people have only been in their house for eighteen months,

> and how they got their fortune nobody knows. They came from Birmingham, which is not a place to promise much, you know. . . . One has not great hopes from Birmingham. . . . they evidently think themselves equal even to my brother Mr. Suckling . . . who has been eleven years a resident at Maple Grove, and whose father had it before him—I believe at least—I am almost sure that old Mr. Suckling had completed the purchase before his death.

In this speech Mrs. Elton, who claims to have 'quite a horror of upstarts', reveals that her own family are only recently in possession of land. She takes every opportunity to boast of Maple Grove, where her sister, Mrs. Suckling, lives. Mrs. Elton is herself an 'upstart' by the old country standards Emma clings to. Maple Grove was bought on mortgage, whereas the gentry inherited estates. Before her marriage, Mrs. Elton had been a Miss Hawkins of Bristol, with £10,000. Her father was a tradesman, just about rich enough to be counted as a merchant. Landed gentry like Emma looked down on commercial Bristol, and Bristol looked down on Birmingham, whose rich set were more recent, less cultured and refined. Birmingham people did not venture to fashionable centres like London or Bath. Miss Hawkins of Bristol met her husband at Bath, and considers herself entitled to sneer at Birmingham.

Bristol fortunes were often made in the slave trade. Mrs. Elton shows herself touchy on this point when Jane Fairfax mentions her own gloomy future as a governess, and an ironically comic scene takes place between them. Jane, of course, is secretly engaged to Frank Churchill and hopes that it will not be necessary to take a job, but she cannot tell anybody this. Jane is made unhappy by Frank's public flirtation with Emma, and Mrs. Elton's officiousness about getting her a job causes her pain, as well as exposing Mrs. Elton's busybody patronizing rudeness. Jane says quietly that when the time comes, she will go to an office in town where inquiry will 'soon produce something—Offices for the sale—not quite of human flesh—but of human intellect'.

Mrs. Elton replies:

> 'Oh! my dear, human flesh! You quite shock me; if you mean a fling at the slave-trade, I assure you Mr. Suckling was always rather a friend to the abolition.'
>
> 'I did not mean, I was not thinking of the slave-trade,' replied Jane; 'governess-trade, I assure you, was all that I had in view; widely different certainly as to the guilt of those who carry it on; but as to the greater misery of the victims, I do not know where it lies. . . .'

Mrs. Elton does not talk about her mercantile father, who may well have made his money in the slave-trade, one way or another; she prefers to boast of her 'brother' (brother-in-law) Mr. Suckling of Maple Grove and his 'barouche-landau', an expensive carriage, a status symbol. It is as if she said 'the Rolls'. Mrs. Elton has the pushy self-assertion of new wealth. It is her fortune, not her talents or qualities of character, which has made her an eligible match.

Emma's snobbery is gently mocked and corrected. In *Persuasion*, however, Jane Austen's last novel, the satire on the 'foolish spendthrift baronet' Sir Walter Elliot and his daughters Mary and Elizabeth is savage, because they claim respect for birth alone. Their moral emptiness is cruelly exposed.

Their friend Lady Russell has persuaded Anne to send away Captain Wentworth, the man Anne loves and who loves her, on the grounds that it would be reckless to marry, at 19, a young naval officer who has yet to make his fortune, causing Anne great unhappiness. Lady Russell is a sympathetic character, but her limitations are clearly marked.

> . . . she had prejudices on the side of ancestry; she had a value for rank and consequence, which blinded her a little to the faults of those who possessed them. She was most correct in her conduct, strict in her notions of decorum, and with manners that were held a standard of good breeding. She had a cultivated mind and was, generally speaking, rational and consistent.

Lady Russell's prejudice on the side of ancestry has nearly disastrous consequences. Yet she is far from negligible; only by the very highest standards is she shown to be wanting. Anne says to her cousin,

> 'My idea of good company, Mr. Elliot, is the company of clever, well-informed people, who have a great deal of conversation; that is what I call good company.'
> 'You are mistaken,' said he gently. 'That is not good company, that is the best. Good company requires only birth, education and manners, and with regard to education is not very nice. Birth and good manners are essential; but a little learning is by no means a dangerous thing in good company, on the contrary it will do very well.'

Mr. Elliot turns out to be a smooth hypocrite, whose pleasant manners conceal a calculating heart. But on social realities we may trust his word. Anne's father, Sir Walter, and her sister Elizabeth, have a 'heartless elegance' which 'gives a general chill'; Elizabeth says 'the proper nothings'. The family are forced to move to Bath, where living is cheaper, and to rent the family estate to a naval officer. Anne is constantly distressed by the heartless snobbery of her father and sisters, who pay servile deference to their grand cousins, the Dalrymples, who belong to the nobility. Anne is embarrassed because she suspects that Viscountess Dalrymple and her daughter consider the Elliots to be pushy bores. Against the cold-hearted formality of the Elliots is set the bluff common sense of Admiral Croft and his wife, who rent Sir Walter's ancestral home from him. Sir Walter is shown as a selfish and irresponsible landowner. Jane Austen shows that she is on the side of feeling, energy and social responsibility against the cold falsity of aristocratic manners at their most meaningless, and the futility of their lifestyle:

> The Mr. Musgroves had their own game to guard, and to destroy; their own horses, dogs and newspapers to engage them; and the females were more fully occupied in all the other common subjects of housekeeping, neighbours, dress, dancing and music.

In this static society, Anne has to find a life for herself. It is she, the spinster, who plays the piano while the others dance. Anne 'had been forced into prudence in her youth, she learned romance as she grew older—the natural sequel of an unnatural beginning'. In giving Anne, her last heroine, a self-made husband, a naval hero like her own brothers, Jane Austen was striking a blow against the static snobberies of people in the same social class as Mr. Darcy and Emma. But Mr. Darcy and Emma, unlike Sir Walter and his daughters, have good hearts and are educated out of their mistakes. Sir Walter, like Shakespeare's King Lear, loses his kingdom through his own folly, and has three daughters, two bad and one who is good.

5

Thackeray:
The Gentleman Clubman

William Makepeace Thackeray (1811–1863) was Dickens's closest rival. Indeed, during their lifetimes, the more fastidious of the reading public respected Thackeray as an artist, while dismissing Dickens as a vulgar hack. Yet Thackeray, born a notch or two higher in the social scale, affected an aristocratic disdain for the way he earned his bread and butter, while Dickens was always the dedicated professional. The men were wary of each other as rivals, though in public each was polite about the other's work.

Thackeray was born in Calcutta, the son and grandson of Indian civil servants. Thackeray's father died when the child was 5, and the young widow remarried two years later. Thackeray was sent to England. The ship stopped at St. Helena, and the boy was taken by a black servant to look at the imprisoned Napoleon. Thackeray went to schools in Hampshire and Chiswick and eventually to Charterhouse, then still on its original site near Smithfield. Thackeray's public school days were not happy ones. His nose was broken in a fight. Thackeray showed no particular promise at school, but towards the end of his schooldays was recognized as a talented author of humorous verse. Aged 17, he left school to be with his mother and her new husband at Larkbeare in Devon, near Ottery St. Mary. In his fictions this becomes 'Clavering St. Mary', Exeter becomes 'Chatteris' and Sidmouth becomes 'Baymouth'. The following year he entered Trinity College, Cambridge, and wrote a poem on Timbuctoo for a journal called the *Snob*, run by town rather than gown. The title was to prove prophetic, for snobs and snobbery, a potent aspect of social relations in Victorian England, were to furnish him with much of his material. Social climbing was regarded by the new entrepreneurial classes, who rose in the wake of the industrial revolution, as a duty to themselves and their heirs. The process was resisted by the traditional aristocracy, who wished to guard their privileges and their hereditary prestige. We have seen this struggle anatomized in the novels of Jane Austen, half a century earlier. Thackeray ranged himself with the gentlefolk, but his own position as the son of an expatriate was not altogether secure, though his family had achieved distinction in army, the law and the church. His son-in-law, Leslie Stephen, wrote in the *Dictionary of National Biography* that Thackeray was an inhabitant of Bohemia under force of distress:

> there meeting many men . . . who were his inferiors in refinement and cultivation. Such people were apt to show their 'unconventionality' by real coarseness, and liked to detect 'snobbishness' in any taste for good society. . . . Thackeray, an intellectual aristocrat though politically a Liberal, was naturally the object of some suspicion to the rougher of his companions. . . . Meanwhile, it was characteristic of his humour that he saw more strongly than any one the bad side of the society which held out to him the strongest temptations. . . .

Thackeray at Cambridge made friends with the future translator of Omar Khayyam, Edward Fitzgerald, Tennyson, A. W. Kinglake (author of *Eothen*) and W. H. Thompson, who was to become Master of their college. But Thackeray was less studious, and finally left Cambridge without a degree, having lost heavily at cards. He wandered to Paris, a city with which he fell in love, and spent the winter of 1830–31 at Weimar, where he met Johann Wolfgang von Goethe (1749–1832), the German philosopher, playwright and poet. This experience of a small German court, which he named Pumpernickel, was put to good use in *Fitzboodle's Confessions* (1842–43) and in his masterpiece, *Vanity Fair* (1847). Returned to England, Thackeray thought of becoming a barrister, and entered the Middle Temple, qualifying in 1848, but never practised. In 1832 he inherited about £20,000, bringing in an income of £500 a year, then a considerable sum, but the money was soon lost in gambling and speculation. He invested in a weekly paper, the *National Standard*, and an Indian bank. The newspaper appears in his fiction as 'The Museum' (*Lovel the Widower*). Thackeray's experiences as a gambler were drawn on in *The Yellowplush Papers* (1837–38), *The Paris Sketchbook* (1840) and in *Pendennis* (Volume two, Chapter five), in the story told by 'Colonel Altamont' to Captain Strong.

By 1834, Thackeray was penniless. He lived in Paris, where life was cheaper, and intended to be an artist. His maternal grandmother moved with him. He worked as a freelance journalist, studying art. He was briefly Paris correspondent of the *Constitutional*, owned by his stepfather. In 1836 he published his first book, *Flore et Zephyr*, a collection of satirical drawings which illustrate the absurdity as well as the beauty of the ballet. Like Clive in *The Newcomes*, he was an accomplished caricaturist and decorative illustrator. He was married in 1836, to Isabella Shaw, daughter of an expatriate Anglo-Irish family. (The Irish are a running joke in Thackeray's work.) She bore him three daughters. The eldest, Anne Isabella, became Lady Ritchie, who wrote novels herself, edited her father's works, and published her memoirs (which included being visited at home by Charlotte Brontë). The second daughter died in infancy (an incident relived in *The Great Hoggarty Diamond*), and the third, Harriet Marian, was Leslie Stephen's first wife. Their mother suffered a permanent mental breakdown. She was in a private mental home in England. The children were sent to their grandmother in Paris. As Trollope put it, Mrs. Thackeray 'became ill and her mind failed her' in 1840, and Thackeray 'became as it were a widower to the end of his days'. Poor Mrs. Thackeray's life dragged on for another fifty-two years.

'Though my marriage was a wreck,' he wrote later, 'I would do it all over again, for behold love is the crown and completion of all earthly good.' Thackeray had married on the strength of his editorship of the *Constitutional*, but when the paper closed a few months later, became a freelance once more. In 1837 Thackeray returned to England, where he reviewed Thomas Carlyle's *The French Revolution* for *The Times*. Carlyle described him as 'a half-monstrous Cornish giant, kind of painter, Cambridge man, and a Paris newspaper correspondent, who is now writing for his life in London. . .'. He became a regular contributor to *Fraser's Magazine*, which first published *The Yellowplush Papers*, supposedly written by a footman called Charles James Yellowplush, who exposed society from the underside. In 1840 Thackeray published *A Shabby-Genteel Story*. The concept of shabby gentility haunts Victorian letters: the book describes the lifestyle of the downwardly mobile, people of some refinement and education struggling to 'keep up appearances' (another key phrase of the period) without enough money and unable to conceal their pinching and scraping. As well as a sharp social observer, Thackeray was also a parodist; his contributions to *Punch* (founded 1840) include brilliant parodies of Sir Walter Scott, Bulwer-Lytton and Disraeli. While the sheer bulk of Thackeray's work is daunting, his wit can still provoke delighted laughter. He wrote, under the name of Michael Angelo Titmarsh, a novella called *The Great Hoggarty Diamond* (1840), which deals with the affairs of the Diddlesex Fire and Insurance Company. The narrator is respected by the clerks because 'I came of a better family than most of them; had received a classical education. . . .' Thackeray pretends to pooh-pooh such advantages, but he and his characters are always conscious of them. Even in such an early work, the dialogue gives sharp insight into the values of contemporary society. Thackeray pays Dickens a delicate compliment in *The Great Hoggarty Diamond*: the hero's wife has her trousseau from 'the celebrated Madame Mantalini of London'. A cautionary tale of speculation and disaster, it has a sequence in debtor's prison. Thackeray's other pen-name was 'George Savage Fitzboodle', in which he assumes the persona of a tobacco-addicted clubman. The story of Deuceace, the gambler in *The Yellowplush Papers*, was, he said, his own, having lost £1,500 at écarté. In 1843 he published *The Irish Sketchbook* and in 1846 *Notes of a Journey from Cornhill to Cairo*.

His Irish experience was used in *The Luck of Barry Lyndon* (1844). Like *The Great Hoggarty Diamond*, this is a moral tale in which the chief character is justly punished. Barry Lyndon, like Fielding's Jonathan Wild, is an anti-hero. Redmond Barry is a rogue who fights a duel and escapes to Dublin, changing his name to Barry Redmond, lives a dissipated life and gets into debt. As a soldier in the Seven Years' War, he fights on both sides, and meets his uncle, Cornelius Barry, calling himself the Chevalier de Balibari. The pair team up as card-sharpers. Eventually, Barry marries a rich widow, the Countess of Lyndon, and changes his name again. He ill-treats his wife and her son and wastes their money. He idolizes his son Bryan, but Bryan is killed in a riding accident. Barry's stepson takes control of his mother's affairs, and Barry is turned into a remittance man. When Lady Lyndon dies, he is reduced to beggary, and dies in the Fleet prison. Stanley Kubrick made a film called *Barry Lyndon* with Ryan O'Neal. Despite alterations in the plot (most notably the suppression of the uncle-nephew relationship between Barry and the Chevalier), the film has great beauty and exquisite traditional music played by Ireland's most distinguished musicians, the Chieftains.

Thackeray contributed a total of 380 sketches to *Punch*, as well as written pieces.

Vanity Fair appeared in 1847. Mrs. Carlyle wrote to her husband that he 'beats Dickens out of the world'. The story is set in the period of the Battle of Waterloo and later. The title reverberates with associations, and should alert us to the fact that the book is a morality. Vanity Fair, in John Bunyan's allegory, *The Pilgrim's Progress* (1678), is where poor Faithful was burnt to death by a worldly and wicked populace. It recalls, too, Ecclesiastes 1:2: 'Vanity of vanities, saith the Preacher, vanity of vanities; all is vanity.' The novel's closing words quote from the Latin of the Vulgate:

> Ah! *Vanitas vanitatum!* which of us is happy in this world? Which of us has his desire? Or, having it, is satisfied?—come children, let us shut up the box and the puppets, for our play is played out.

The narrative is framed, by a 'Before the curtain' note written in 1848, in the central metaphor of the world as a fair, in which there is a

great quantity of eating and drinking, making love and jilt-
ing, laughing and the contrary, smoking, cheating, fighting,
dancing and fiddling . . . knaves picking pockets. . . . Yes,
this is VANITY FAIR; not a moral place certainly; nor a
merry one, though very noisy. Look at the faces of the
actors and buffoons when they come off from their business. . . .

The author likens himself to the manager of a show, who
disclaims a moral. 'Some people consider Fairs immoral
altogether, and eschew such, with their servants and their
families: very likely they are right.' Thackeray here glances
at the puritans, such as Carlyle's father, who considered all
fiction as 'immoral', because it was not true. But *Vanity Fair*
is nonetheless a secular morality, based on the medieval concept of the world as stage. Like Jonathan Swift, Thackeray is
a master of irony, and none of his explicit statements should
be taken at face value without examination. The words of
D. H. Lawrence are relevant: 'Never trust the teller, trust the
tale.' The tension, however, between tale and teller is a major
component of Thackeray's art. His pretence at detachment,
derived from his beloved Fielding, has misled readers into
thinking that he despised his own tale, along with his characters. Yet he tells us clearly enough, for example in Chapter 8,
what he is about:

> . . . my kind reader will please to remember that this history
> has *Vanity Fair* for a title, and that Vanity Fair is a very vain,
> wicked, foolish place, full of all sorts of humbugs and false-
> nesses and pretensions. . . . one is bound to speak the truth
> as far as one knows it, whether one mounts a cap and bells
> or a shovel hat . . . [the shovel hat was the secular mark of a
> bishop].

While Christian, in Bunyan's fable, completes his journey,
Faithful is the hero martyred at Vanity Fair. In the novel,
Dobbin plays the role of Faithful; he does not die, but his
reward is too petty for his deserts.

The novel opens at a demure girls' school in Chiswick,
where rich, pampered Amelia Sedley is leaving for home,
accompanied by the French instructor, Rebecca Sharp, on her
way to become a governess.

Miss Rebecca was not . . . in the least kind or placable. All the world used her ill, said this young misanthropist, and we may be certain that persons whom all the world treats ill, deserve entirely the treatment they get. The world is a looking-glass and gives back to every man the reflection of his own face.

Critics have tried to argue that Becky is 'good-humoured' because Thackeray calls her so, but we are warned early that she is a 'dangerous bird'. Rebecca's background is not respectable: her father was a drunken artist, and her mother a French opera girl (Victorian shorthand for 'loose woman'). 'The humble calling of her female parent Miss Sharp never alluded to . . .', Rebecca was consumed by envy of the privileged boarders, but latches on to Amelia. Rebecca immediately sets her cap at Amelia's rich bachelor brother, the gross Joseph Sedley, Collector of Boggley Wallah in India, but he escapes her clutches. Amelia becomes engaged to George Osborne, a shallow and vain young man, but when Amelia's father loses all his money, George wants to jilt her. George's schoolfriend William Dobbin, in love with Amelia himself, persuades George to marry Amelia secretly. In consequence, George is disinherited. Rebecca secretly hates George Osborne for warning Jos Sedley about her designs on him. Meanwhile, Rebecca has been working for the family of Sir Pitt Crawley, an uncouth baronet who derives in part from Squire Western in Fielding's *Tom Jones*. She ingratiates herself with Sir Pitt's sister, Miss Crawley, an aristocratic lady with left-wing views. On the death of his wife, Sir Pitt proposes marriage to Becky, but she replies, 'Oh, Sir Pitt! I am married already!' She has married Sir Pitt's younger son, Rawdon. The democratic Miss Crawley disinherits her nephew for marrying an upstart, and the couple are forced to live on their wits, not paying bills. Rawdon becomes a professional gambler.

All three young men are in the army, and gather together with Amelia and Becky in Belgium on the night before Waterloo. George is left on the field, with a bullet through his heart. Prostrated, Amelia returns to her parents and gives birth to a son, Georgy, whom she idolizes as the image of her adored late husband. Dobbin proposes marriage, but Amelia refuses, shocked. Dobbin goes off to India for twelve years.

Amelia is sweet but insipid and foolish, and her silliness is criticized within the novel. Old Mr. Osborne persuades Amelia to give up her son (whose character is as unpleasant as his late father's) for education and the advantages that money can give. Meanwhile, Becky and Rawdon climb higher and higher in society, with no visible means of support. She is even presented to George IV, '. . . there too was Vanity'. Throughout the novel, there is a play on the two meanings of the word vanity: futility and vain conceit. The novel is about the worthlessness of appearances and the value of true and loving hearts. Becky now treats her husband with contempt, though he loves and admires her; she also neglects their son, little Rawdy. At Waterloo, Rawdon and Becky were subsidized by an elderly General, but Rebecca stoutly denied there was anything improper in the association. Rawdon is arrested for debt, and when his kind sister-in-law, Lady Jane, gets him out of debtor's prison, comes home to find Rebecca with the rich, dissolute Marquis of Steyne (read 'Stain').

> The wretched woman was in full toilette, her arms and all her fingers sparkling with bracelets and rings, and the brilliants on her breast that Steyne had given her. . . . 'I am innocent, Rawdon,' she said, 'before God, I am innocent . . . Say I am innocent,' she said to Lord Steyne. . . .
>
> 'You innocent! Damn you,' he screamed out. 'You innocent, when every trinket you have on your body is paid for by me. I have given you thousands of pounds which this fellow has spent and for which he has sold you.'

Rawdon tells Becky to take off her jewels. 'He tore the diamond ornament out of her breast and flung it at Lord Steyne. It cut him on his bald forehead. . . .' Rawdon leaves her without a word. The novelist asks us: 'What *had* happened? Was she guilty or not? She said not, but who could tell . . . if that corrupt heart was in this case pure?' We know, of course, that she was not innocent; when Lord Steyne says 'every trinket on your body is paid for by me', we hear, 'your body has been paid for by me'. Rawdon realizes that Becky had plotted to have him arrested, so he would be out of the way.

The servants leave and society closes its ranks against

Becky. Rawdon is offered the governorship of the Coventry Islands. Rebecca goes abroad. The innuendo about her 'virtue' is resumed in Chapter 64:

> We must pass over a part of Mrs. Rebecca Crawley's biography with that lightness and delicacy which the world demands—the moral world, that has, perhaps no particular objection to vice, but an insuperable repugnance to hearing vice called by its proper name. There are things we do and know perfectly well in Vanity Fair, though we never speak of them: as the Ahrimanians worship the devil, but don't mention him: and a polite public will no more bear to read an authentic description of vice than a truly refined English or American female will permit the word breeches to be pronounced in her chaste hearing. . . . I defy anyone to say that Becky, who has certainly some vices, has not been presented to the public in a perfectly genteel and inoffensive manner. In describing this Siren, singing and smiling, coaxing and cajoling, the author, with modest pride, asks his readers all round, has he once forgotten the laws of politeness and showed the monster's hideous tail above water? No! Those who like may peep down under waves that are pretty transparent and see it writhing and twirling, diabolically hideous and slimy, flapping amongst bones, or curling round corpses; but above the waterline, I ask, has not everything been proper, agreeable and decorous, and has any the most squeamish immoralist in Vanity Fair a right to cry fie? When, however, the Siren disappears and dives below, down among the dead men, the water of course grows turbid over her, and it is labour lost to look into it ever so curiously. They look pretty enough when they sit on a rock, twanging their harps and combing their hair, and sing, and beckon to you to come and hold the looking glass; but when they sink into their native element, depend on it, those mermaids are about no good, and we had best not examine the fiendish marine cannibals, revelling and feasting on their wretched pickled victims. And so, when Becky is out of the way, be sure that she is not particularly well employed, and that the less that is said about her doings is in fact the better.

Now what is all that about? The clue is surely in 'tail', which since at least the time of Shakespeare has had ribald connotations. Becky presents an attractive figure above the waterline (the waist), but what goes on below is horrible.

As a Cambridge undergraduate I remember arguing that this passage both attacks Victorian hypocrisy and tells us that Becky graduates from being a kept woman to being a common prostitute. My supervisor, Mrs. Q. D. Leavis (who thought Thackeray an undistinguished writer anyway), was shocked and angry at such an indecent suggestion. Fortunately for my self-esteem, A. E. Dyson published an essay in *Critical Quarterly* that very month, arguing for the same case as mine.

Becky becomes slatternly and addicted to brandy, though the 'degradation did not take place all at once'. Becky drifts about Europe, gambling with men 'in her private room'. She receives a death threat from Lord Steyne. In Pumpernickel, Jos Sedley turns up. Rebecca insures his life and he dies soon afterwards in mysterious circumstances. Before he dies, however, Jos tries to persuade the returned Dobbin of Becky's innocence and brings Amelia to see her. Becky convinces Amelia that she is an injured woman, whose husband has left her, taken her child away and left her to sing for her living. Dobbin tries to warn her, but Amelia is obstinate. Becky tells Amelia she should marry Dobbin and Amelia snivels about George. Becky tells Amelia that George was 'weary of you, and would have jilted you, but that Dobbin forced him to keep his word. . . . He never cared for you. . . . He . . . made love to me the week after he married you!' and Becky takes out of her belt the note George wrote her before he was shot, proposing an elopement. This incident is seized on by Becky's defenders to show she has generosity. I would argue rather that the plot demands it (and why should Rebecca keep a note from George all those years and happen to have it with her?). Becky, like Swift's yahoos and Milton's Satan, though evil, has all the life, while loving plodders like Dobbin represent patient merit spurned by the unworthy. Dobbin marries Amelia, and is disappointed. Rebecca ends her days calling herself Lady Crawley, though Rawdon has died too soon to make her so, haunting churches and charitable organizations. Her son inherits the title and refuses to see his mother, paying her to stay away. He regards his paternal aunt, Lady Jane Crawley, as his mother. Just as Dobbin is the true hero, Lady Jane, principled and loving, is the true heroine. The imagery throughout is of brilliance and sparkle, true and false lights.

Thackeray has been accused of cynicism on the one hand and sentimentality on the other. Dr. Gordon Ray, Thackeray's biographer, has argued that Thackeray's marriage was less happy than Thackeray admitted, and that Amelia is a portrait of the weakminded Mrs. Thackeray. As evidence, he believes that Thackeray idealizes Amelia at the start of the story and patronizes her at the end. But the novel establishes at once that Amelia is good but too trusting, while Rebecca is hard and vindictive. As to the cynicism, his audience recognized that Thackeray was writing about a demi-mondaine. Thackeray's string of apparently innocent questions as to what 'really' happened is a strategy for coping with Victorian prudery. He hints expertly at unpleasant facts; we learn from the information that old Sir Pitt became helpless and had to be 'fed and cleaned like a baby'—that Sir Pitt became incontinent. Thackeray regretted the loss of the previous century's frankness. In the preface to *Pendennis*, dated 26 November 1850, he wrote: 'Since the author of *Tom Jones* was buried, no writer of fiction among us has been permitted to depict to his utmost power a MAN.' The overcoming of this difficulty has led to much misreading, but in *Vanity Fair* Thackeray shows a fine moral poise and a masterly, playful, control of tone. Becky's is a Rake's Progress.

Thackeray worshipped his mother, though her love for him would seem to have been rather stifling. *Pendennis* is semi-autobiographical, about a young man who has his way to make in the world. Arthur Pendennis is touchy about being the grandson of a mere medical man (for doctors had lower social prestige in the early nineteenth century than lawyers, clergymen and soldiers, because of their association with apothecaries and barber-surgeons). Like the young Thackeray, Pendennis is the son of a sweet-natured widow. As young men will, Pendennis falls unwisely in love. His lady is an actress, 'Miss Fotheringay', whose real name is Emily Costigan. Pendennis has a kindly uncle who gets him out of trouble by persuading the lady's father, Captain Costigan, that Arthur has no money. An actress, at that time, was scarcely more respectable than an opera dancer. Putting this youthful folly behind him, Pendennis goes to the University of 'Oxbridge', where he gets into debt. He pays off this burden with the help of a loan from his mother's adopted daughter, Laura Bell. Helen wistfully hopes that Laura and Arthur will marry, but Arthur obstinately falls in love with another unsuitable young woman. Blanche Amory seems to be well-connected, as her mother is Lady Clavering, wife of Sir Francis. But Blanche is affected and false, and her mother vulgar, though rich. Major Pendennis, the uncle, discovers the shameful family secret: Blanche's father, Lady Clavering's first husband, is still alive, and is blackmailing the Clavering family. Yet Major Pendennis encourages Pendennis's romance with Blanche.

Intending to read for the bar, Pendennis moves to London. He gets a foothold in the literary world when George Warrington, who is in the same chambers, introduces young Arthur to the editor of a new magazine, the *Pall Mall Gazette*. Captain Shandon, however, is in debtor's prison, and is editing the journal from there, which would seem to be inconvenient. Pendennis becomes involved with another girl, Fanny Bolton. Fanny belongs to the working class. Pendennis falls ill and Fanny nurses him. Arthur's mother assumes that Fanny must be her son's mistress, and harshly rejects her. So furious is Arthur that he threatens to marry Fanny. But he is warned off by Warrington, who has married in haste and repented at leisure. Abandoned by Pendennis, Fanny marries a medical student. Blanche still has her claws into Arthur, who feels he should stick with her out of duty, after the family skeleton in the cupboard is revealed. However, Blanche is faithless and turns Arthur down for the son of a rich brewer, leaving him free to marry Laura, Helen having died.

Thackeray never surpassed the achievement of *Vanity Fair*, though for many years his historical novel, *The History of Henry Esmond* (1852) was considered his finest work. If the mother-figure in *Pendennis* is ambivalently treated, in *Esmond* the hero marries one. It is a melancholy story of disappointed love, reflecting the end of Thackeray's frustrated relationship with Jane Brookfield, the wife of a college friend. The Brookfields were not happily married, and Thackeray lost both friends at the same time, due to the husband's jealousy and the wife's fit of conscience. The story is set in the early eighteenth century. The hero spends a lonely childhood among Jacobites, believing himself to be an illegitimate son of a Viscount Castlewood, who was killed at the Battle of the Boyne in 1690. Henry's cousin Francis Esmond has the title, is married to Rachel and is the father of two children, Frank and Beatrix. They treat Henry with kindness, but without meaning to he brings an infection of smallpox, so that Rachel loses her beauty, which alienates her husband. Rachel pays for young Esmond to go to Cambridge University, whence he returns to find the wicked Lord Mohun almost living in the house, gambling with the husband and harassing the wife. There is a duel between the two titled gentlemen and Castlewood is killed. On Francis's deathbed, Henry is given a written confession that the title is not his, but Henry's, for Henry is legitimate after all. Henry, out of gratitude, and wanting Frank to inherit because the family have been so good to him, burns this paper. For conniving at the duel, Henry goes to prison. Rachel withdraws her approval, angrily. Once out of prison, Henry goes abroad to fight in the War of the Spanish Succession. He comes home and falls in love with the haughty, whimsical Beatrix (a character who fascinates Thackeray and, apparently, many male readers, but is rather irritating to female ones). Henry longs for this proud beauty when he is not fighting for the Duke of Marlborough abroad; he misses none of the action, fighting at Blenheim and Ramillies, and discovers that his mother was a Flamande buried in Brussels. Beatrix, on the pinnacle of social success, becomes engaged to the Duke of Hamilton, but this nobleman, like Beatrix's father, fights with Lord Mohun. This time both are killed. Beatrix confesses to Henry that she did not love her fiancé.

> . . . I think I have no heart; at least, I have never seen the man that could touch it; and, had I found him, I would have followed him in rags had he been a private soldier, or to sea, like one of those buccaneers you used to read to us about when we were children. I would do anything for such a man, bear anything for him: but I never found one. You were ever too much of a slave to win my heart; even my Lord Duke could not command it. I had not been happy

had I married him. I knew that three months after our engagement, and was too vain to break it. . . . I am not good, Harry: my mother is gentle and good like an angel.

(Beatrix is heartless very much like Estella in *Great Expectations* eight years later, but there is no reason for Beatrix's hard selfishness. Estella's, on the other hand, is psychologically motivated by the conditioning given her by crazed, vengeful Miss Havisham.) After the death of Hamilton, Beatrix offers Esmond her diamonds, which he refuses, and talks of becoming a nun. Kissed, her 'cheek was as cold as marble'. Beatrix is fiercely Jacobite, and Henry joins in a plot to restore to the throne 'King James III', the Old Pretender (1688–1766), when Queen Anne dies in 1714. However, royalty neglects politics to run after Beatrix, and loses the loyalty of Esmond and his cousin Frank. Beatrix offers her love to Esmond, but it is too late. 'I have never seen her from that day.' Beatrix has turned against her family and fled to France. Esmond, astonishingly, realizes that he has always been in love with her mother, anyway.

Esmond had great success initially. But soon there was a slashing review in *The Times*, and critics began to complain that the pace was slow, the tone melancholy, and the love story unpleasant. Thackeray decided it was no use struggling to write his best for a public who were unappreciative. He decided he would try and write for the popular taste. He felt he was 'worked out', 'too old for story-telling', and that the book was not an advance on his previous works. Yet although he rated *Esmond* higher, *The Newcomes* is in my view his most entertaining book, apart from *Vanity Fair* and *The Book of Snobs*.

Thackeray wrote, during its composition, that

> it goes pretty well: like the other yellow books—not so high-toned or so carefully finished as Esmond but that you see was a failure besides being immoral. We must take pains and write careful books . . . for the young ladies.

Colonel Newcome was modelled on Henry Carmichael-Smith, Thackeray's own stepfather. Arthur Pendennis is the narrator of *The Newcomes* (1853–55). Colonel Thomas Newcome, who has spent most of his life in India, is a widower and a good man, something of an innocent, quite different from his rich and pretentious half-brothers. Colonel Newcome's son Clive is sent home to England to go to school. The father comes home from India when Clive is in his teens. Clive is in love with his cousin Ethel, daughter of Sir Brian Newcome, but Ethel's relations are ambitious for her and want her to make a splendid marriage with another cousin, Lord Kew. Although Ethel is a girl of spirit, it is difficult for a girl of her position not to submit to the pressure of the marriage-market, and she does agree to marry Lord Kew. The marriage does not, however, take place, and Ethel becomes engaged once more, to Lord Farintosh. But Ethel sees the appalling marriage of her uncle Barnes Newcome, whose wife is driven to run away. This grim example influences Ethel to give up the idea of marriage altogether. Clive has meanwhile married somebody else. Colonel Newcome's fortune is lost when a bank collapses, and the family are reduced to poverty. Clive's mother-in-law makes his life a misery for the poor old Colonel, who dies. Clive's wife, too, dies, so Clive and Ethel are both free.

Colonel Newcome is good-hearted, and shocked by the worldliness and superficiality of his rich relatives. Like Dobbin, he is a victim of his own goodness and the acquisitiveness of other people. Recurrent preoccupations in Thackeray's fiction are the difficulty of marrying the right person, gambling, debt, and the failure of banks: all these reflect Thackeray's own life-experience.

Unlike Dickens, Thackeray was happy on his visits to America. *The Virginians*, a sequel to *Esmond*, was published 1857–59. The Esmond family have emigrated to Virginia. A generation later, Esmond and Rachel have twin grandsons, George and Henry Warrington, in America and in England. The boys look alike, but are very different in personality. Their mother, also called Rachel (daughter of Esmond and the older Rachel) pets Harry, who is cheerful and attractive, and is harsh with his brother George, who is scholarly and serious. The boys, however, are good friends. George, who is the elder, and thus the heir to the title of Viscount Castlewood, disappears after an attack on the French. As George is thought to be dead, Harry is now the heir. He visits England and meets his Castlewood relations. Harry is an innocent Colonial boy, and is soon led into bad courses by the wicked Europeans, who lead him into gambling and trap him into an engagement with a cousin, Maria, who is much older than he is. Like Sammy Titmarsh in *The Great Hoggarty Diamond*, Rawdon Crawley and others, Harry is arrested for debt. But good George turns up from the dead and Maria no longer wants to marry Harry, as the money will be George's after all. George's mother is ambitious for him, and wants him to marry American money. Instead, George obstinately marries Theo, a soldier's daughter, and his mother cuts off the money supply. Sir Miles Warrington, another relative, comes forward to rescue him. The haughty and capricious Beatrix Esmond is now the worldly old Baroness Bernstein, and she leaves Harry money in her will. Harry is with Wolfe at the capture of Quebec. Theo's sister, George's sister-in-law, Hetty Lambert, is in love with Harry, but Harry marries his mother's housekeeper's daughter, Fanny Mountain, instead. Harry joins George Washington when the American War of Independence breaks out. George is in the British army, and is so horrified at the thought of fighting his own brother that he resigns his commission. He gives up the Virginia property to Harry and settles on the Warrington family estate in England.

Thomas Carlyle wrote to Ralph Waldo Emerson in 1853:

> Thackeray . . . is a big fellow, soul and body; of many gifts and qualities (particularly in the Hogarth line, with a dash of Sterne superadded), of enormous *appetite* withal, and very uncertain and chaotic in all points except his *outer breeding*, which is fixed enough and *perfect*, according to the modern English style I rather dread explosions in his history. A *big*, fierce, weeping, hungry man; not a strong one.

The same writer told Monckton Milnes after Thackeray died:

> He had many fine qualities, no guile or malice against any mortal; a big mass of a soul, but not strong in proportion; a beautiful vein of genius lay struggling about him. . . .

Anthony Trollope wrote:

> I regard him as one of the most tender-hearted human

beings I ever knew, who, with an exaggerated contempt for the foibles of the world at large, would entertain an almost equally exaggerated sympathy with the joys and troubles of individuals around him.

Thackeray was six feet three inches tall, his head was massive, and his brain was said to weigh 58½ ounces.

6

Charles Dickens: Panorama of Nineteenth-century London

Charles John Huffham Dickens (1812–70) is one of England's greatest writers. His novels show compassion for the poor, humour, a wonderful ear for dialogue, and the imagination of a poet, which shows itself in powerful symbolic imagery; his talent is fertile and exuberant.

Dickens was born in Portsmouth, on the southern coast of England, and later lived in the dockyard town of Chatham. His father, John Dickens, was a clerk in the Navy Pay Office, but got into financial difficulties. He was imprisoned for debt in the Marshalsea prison, now demolished. It is said that Dickens portrayed his father as a figure of comedy in *David Copperfield* (1849–50) and as a figure of tragedy in *Little Dorrit* (1855–57).

Young Charles was a precocious reader, and as a child browsed among the literature of the previous century, such as Daniel Defoe's *Robinson Crusoe* (1719), Tobias Smollett's *Roderick Random* (1748), Henry Fielding's *Tom Jones* (1749), and Oliver Goldsmith's *The Vicar of Wakefield* (1766), as well as *The Arabian Nights*. His novels combine everyday realism with a romantic sense of the wonderful.

Charles was the second of eight children, an under-sized and sickly lad. His mother taught him to read and even a little Latin. Charles and his sister Fanny went to a 'dame school', in which an unqualified old woman taught children elementary reading, writing and arithmetic. This was a common arrangement at the time. He also went to the local theatre.

When Dickens was 10, his father was transferred to Camden Town, now part of central London, but in those days separated from the city by fields. Dickens's sister went on a scholarship to the Royal Academy of Music, but there was no school for Charles, who complained later that his father had at this time apparently

> utterly lost . . . the idea of educating me at all. . . . So I degenerated into cleaning his boots of a morning . . . and going on such poor errands as arose out of our poor way of living.

(Little Dorrit's elder sister Fanny is spoilt, selfish and snobbish, in contrast to the self-sacrificing Amy herself.)

A family friend, James Lamert, offered Charles a job, when he was 12, in a boot-blacking factory. The boy was bitterly angry. Later he wrote:

> It is wonderful to me how I could have been so easily cast away at such an age. It is wonderful to me, that, even after my descent into the poor little drudge I had been since we came to London, no one had compassion enough on me—a child of singular abilities, quick, eager, delicate, and soon hurt, bodily or mentally—to suggest that something might have been spared, as certainly it might have been, to place me at any common school. Our friends, I take it, were tired out. No one made any sign. My father and mother were quite satisfied. They could hardly have been more so, if I had been twenty years of age, distinguished at a grammar school, and going to Cambridge.

The lack of a university education rankled all his life, though in the words of G. K. Chesterton (1874–1936), he was 'a man without culture, without tradition, without help from historic religions or philosophies or from the great foreign schools', yet with 'a naked flame of mere natural genius'. Dickens blamed his parents, but they needed his earnings of 6s. (30p) a week. Most boys worked as he did, from eight in the morning till eight at night, but Dickens had been brought up to expect better things, despite his family's financial instability. A recurrent theme in Dickens is that of the clerk whose family is too large and whose income is too small. Originally Dickens worked on his own, in the rotting warehouse, noisy with rats, putting the paper caps on the bottles, and paste on their printed labels. His separate table was eventually moved into the general workroom, where Dickens despised the rough boys he worked with. They mocked him as 'the young gentleman'. Dickens said later:

> No words can express the secret agony of my soul as I sunk into this companionship; compared these every day associates with those of my happier childhood; and felt my early hopes of growing up to be a learned and distinguished man, crushed in my breast. The deep remembrance of the sense I had of being utterly neglected and hopeless; of the shame I felt in my position; of the misery it was to my young heart to believe that, day by day, what I had learned and thought, and delighted in, and raised my fancy and my emulation up by, was passing away from me, never to be brought back any more; cannot be written. My whole nature was so penetrated with the grief and humiliation of such considerations, that even now, famous and caressed and happy, I often forget in my dreams that I have a dear wife and children; even that I am a man; and wander desolately back to that time of my life.

And a few days after Charles was put to work, his father was arrested. Young Dickens thought his heart was broken. His father told him to take warning by the Marshalsea, and to observe that if a man had £20.0s.0d. a year, and spent £19.19s.6d., he would be happy; but that a shilling spent the other way would make him wretched. This observation later became immortal on the lips of Mr. Micawber in *David Copperfield*. Meanwhile, Mrs. Dickens pawned all the family possessions. Mrs. Dickens and the younger children moved into the prison to live. The debtors could not leave, but their families could go in and out until the gates were locked at night. John Dickens was receiving sick pay from the Navy Post Office, but Charles, out at work, went into lodgings. His landlady turns up in *Dombey and Son* as the grim Mrs. Pipchin. The Dickens servant in happier times was called Mary Weller and one of the young Dickens's workmates was Bob Fagin, names that he used in *The Pickwick Papers* (1837) and in *Oliver*

Twist (1837–38). The observant child grew up into a novelist who wasted nothing.

Inside the prison, John Dickens was chairman of the prisoners' committee. His mother died and her legacy cleared his debts. He spent three months in the Marshalsea; Dickens leaves Mr. Dorrit there for over twenty years. John Dickens went back to his job and Charles expected to be released from his. The warehouse had moved to Covent Garden and Charles was set to work in the window, where people gathered to watch the speed with which he and Bob Fagin did their work. One day Dickens saw his father outside, and wondered how he could bear it. Indeed, John Dickens did not put up with it, and took Charles away, promising to send him to school. Dickens's mother wanted the boy sent back at once to continue earning. The boy never forgave her. This early drudgery was a bitter secret. He was in the blacking warehouse for four months. He exaggerated this experience in *David Copperfield*. The anguish burnt into his memory and made him hard-working and ambitious. Irresponsible parents and suffering children recur throughout his novels. As Chesterton wrote:

> Though his characters often were caricatures, they were not such wild caricatures as was supposed by those who had never met such characters. And the critics had never met the characters; because the critics did not live in the common life of the English people; and Dickens did. England was a much more amusing and horrible place than it appeared to the sort of man who wrote reviews. . . . Dickens drew reels and reels of highly coloured caricature out of an ordinary person, as dazzlingly as a conjuror draws reels and reels of highly coloured paper out of an ordinary hat.

The art critic John Ruskin (1819–1900) said that though Dickens's caricature might be gross, it was never mistaken.

Dickens spent a couple of years at school, then worked as a messenger, learning shorthand in his spare time. He was a 'workaholic' and in his tales he treats with contempt the idler, the drop-out, the young man who will not stick at a trade. Examples are Richard Carstone and Harold Skimpole in *Bleak House* (1852–53), and Tip Dorrit in *Little Dorrit*. Soon

Dickens was earning a living as a freelance reporter of court cases.

He fell in love with a girl called Maria Beadnell, whose parents did not consider him good enough for their daughter. Maria flirted with him, teased him and finally refused him. Dickens did not see her for twenty years, and when he met her again she had lost her looks. The pretty, flirtatious girl had become a fat, simpering middle-aged woman, whose limitations were cruelly exposed, now her looks had gone. Dickens portrayed her as the good-hearted but sentimental, incoherent and absurd Flora Finching in *Little Dorrit* (which George Bernard Shaw (1856–1950) considered to be Dickens's masterpiece). Dickens showed Flora as kindly, but ridiculous. 'Flora, whom he had left a lily, had become a peony.' The real Maria was now married, with a daughter; Flora Finching still sighs hopelessly for Arthur Clennam.

In 1831, when Dickens was 19, he was offered a job as reporter on the *Mirror of Parliament*, a journal like *Hansard*, which gave verbatim reports of parliamentary proceedings. Dickens soon made his mark as a brilliant reporter, a fast and accurate shorthand writer. He regarded Parliament as corrupt and inefficient. In Dickens's eyes, the country was run by the Coodles and the Doodles, the Buffeys and the Duffeys, the old privileged families, ultra-conservative, whose influence was stultifying: they are stigmatized in *Little Dorrit* as being in charge of the Circumlocution Office. The new men were commercial go-getters, crooks lacking in public spirit. Dickens called Parliament the national dust-heap (a euphemism for piles of refuse and night-soil, which in Dickens's time was emptied into the streets). In 1832, Parliament was reformed so that the vote was no longer restricted to the aristocratic classes. However, universal adult suffrage for men and women on equal terms did not come till 1929.

In his twenties, Dickens was making money by writing about the life he knew, the working people and the middle-class people of London. He is the first novelist to set his work not in the country, with occasional forays to the metropolis, but in and around the Great Wen, as William Cobbett (1763–1845) called it. But Dickens's success was spoiled by his always having to rescue his improvident father from debt.

Dickens married Catherine Hogarth in 1836, when he was 24. The marriage was not happy, as Mrs. Dickens was sluggish whereas her husband was active and mercurial. Dickens was deeply attached to his young sister-in-law, Mary Hogarth, who lived with the couple, and who died suddenly in 1837 at the age of 18. Dickens never got over the shock, and she reappears in several of the novels as the young, innocent, suffering heroine.

When Dickens was 25, his short stories were collected into *The Pickwick Papers*, the book that made him rich and famous. He started writing serials for various publishers, several at once. All his life the pace of work put a strain on his health, despite his enormous vital energies, and finally overwork killed him.

Dickens is best understood in the light of fairy-tale archetypes. G. K. Chesterton called Dickens, 'A mythologist rather than a novelist. . .'. The melodrama for which he has been criticized is the stuff of the European folk-tale; his stories are full of ogres, distressed damsels, rescuers, and the setting is not the traditional one of the countryside, but nineteenth-century London, evoked in all its teeming energy and squalor. Dickens's characters belong in the main to the lower and lower middle class, whose speech Dickens records and recreates with the accuracy and inventiveness of a master. The incoherent and ungrammatical ramblings of people like Flora Finching (*Little Dorrit*) and Nicholas Nickleby's mother can be heard today by the alert eavesdropper.

Professor Philip Collins has written two excellent books, which any serious student of Dickens should read: *Dickens and Crime* (1962) and *Dickens and Education* (1963).

Oliver Twist, Dickens's first complete novel, has passed into British mythology, so that everybody is expected to recognize cartoon characters holding up a bowl as referring to the incident in the workhouse when Oliver, the charity boy, dares to ask for a second helping of gruel. The story has achieved even more widespread popularity through the medium of Lionel Bart's brilliant musical, *Oliver!*

Jewish readers were distressed by the depiction of Fagin, often referred to in the narrative as 'the Jew'. In order to correct this vicious stereotype, Dickens eventually compensated by creating the noble and generous Mr. Riah in *Our Mutual Friend*.

In 1839 *Nicholas Nickleby* was published. Nicholas goes as a schoolmaster to Dotheboys Hall, a school where unwanted children are brutally ill-treated. Yorkshire schools were a notorious disgrace, and in those days of bad roads and slow coaches children put to school in Yorkshire were well out of the way. Dickens and his illustrator, Hablot K. Browne ('Phiz'), made a special investigative trip to Greta Bridge, in North Yorkshire, to see conditions for themselves. The novel is set three miles from Greta Bridge.

Barnaby Rudge (1840) was about the Gordon riots, with a lunatic for a mascot, and *The Old Curiosity Shop* (1841) is chiefly remembered for Quilp, the dwarf, a sly, cunning and ferocious man, and Little Nell, who lives with her grandfather, a gambler who gets into Quilp's moneylending clutches. Reduced to beggary, Little Nell dies. Readers pleaded with Dickens, as they had pleaded with Samuel Richardson, not to let his heroine die. John Ruskin said Little Nell had been butchered for the market; Oscar Wilde (1854–1900) said one would have to have a heart of stone not to laugh at the death of Little Nell. The novel is not greatly admired today, but was an enormous success in its time.

Martin Chuzzlewit (1843–44) incorporated Dickens's (not altogether favourable) impressions of America, where the author sends his hero for a spell, after Martin loses his job. At the same time, he produced *A Christmas Carol*, enduringly popular, with its reformed miser, Scrooge, frightened by Marley's ghost, the pathetic child cripple, Tiny Tim, and his struggling father, Bob Cratchit. The book celebrates generosity and jollity and renewal, the replacing of a heart of stone by a heart of flesh.

Dombey and Son (1847–48) was the first of the novels on which Dickens's current reputation rests. It is the story of a rejected daughter, who finally returns to be reconciled with her father (indeed, the plot has affinities with *King Lear*, except that there is a happy ending). Dombey has been described as first railway novel, and Professor Raymond Williams suggested that Tolstoy had been influenced by *Dombey* when he plotted *Anna Karenina* some thirty years later. At the end of Chapter 16, when Paul dies, Miss Tox, the kindly old spinster, weeps: '. . . To think that Dombey and Son should be a Daughter after all!' This is the main theme of the novel, and was inexplicably omitted from all editions of the book after 1858, except for reprints of the first edition. The Penguin English Library edition, with its introduction by Raymond Williams, is recommended.

If *Dombey* is the first novel about business, *David Copperfield* (1849) was the first of Dickens's novels in which he mined and transmuted his childhood. It was Dickens's own favourite among his books. The hero, who grows up to be a novelist, is the child of a widowed mother. When David's mother marries the cruel Mr. Murdstone, who is abetted by a spinster sister, David's happiness is over. His beloved but feeble mother falls under the Murdstone influence, and David is sent away to school, where he is miserable. His mother dies, and David is put to menial employment. Dickens here transmutes his real father's abrogation of responsibility into death; the father's place is taken by a cruel interloper (the cousin who gave young Dickens a job?), and the mother is helpless. John Dickens is kindly immortalized as the improvident, but ever-optimistic, father of David's substitute family, the Micawbers, with whom David lodges. Mr. Micawber, like John Dickens, is imprisoned for debt. In *David Copperfield* Dickens regains the narrative pace and the brilliant characterization of *Nicholas Nickleby*, though the earlier part, dealing with David's childhood, is by far the most vivid.

Bleak House appeared in monthly parts from 1852–53. Contemporaries received it coolly, but in this century it has frequently been considered Dickens's masterpiece. Its opening description of London fog, mud and soot, is famous:

> Smoke lowering down from the chimney-pots, making a soft black drizzle with flakes of soot in it as big as full-grown snowflakes—gone into mourning, one might imagine, for the death of the sun. . . . Fog everywhere. Fog up the river, where it flows among green aits and meadows; fog down the river where it rolls defiled among the tiers of shipping, and the waterside pollutions of a great (and dirty) city. . . .

While industrial pollution was one of the pressing anxieties of the mid-nineteenth century, Dickens's fog is symbolic.

The plot and symbolism are complex, but the main target of Dickens's satire is the cumbersome process of English law, which benefits only the legal profession. This is epitomized in the career of Richard Carstone, who fritters his life waiting for settlement of a lawsuit which will bring him an inheritance. But by the time the suit drags to its end, all the money has been consumed in costs.

Hard Times (1854) is also sombre, a tragic picture of industrial Britain. Its attack on Utilitarianism, economic individualism and *laissez-faire* capitalism is less political than romantic; the soul of England can only be saved by the values embodied in the circus (spontaneous enjoyment and true feeling). Radicalism has been identified with economic individualism, but Dickens, like others who wrote at that time on the 'condition of England', parted from the Radicals in putting forward a programme not of social reform but of spiritual renewal; the solution they demanded was impracticable, considering the prevailing conditions, which could only be helped by legislation. Macaulay, however, condemned the novel for its 'sullen socialism', though for most twentieth-century readers the book is not socialist enough. The sly portrait of the windbag Trade Union leader Slackbridge as an unscrupulous self-seeker has been influential in the subsequent fictional treatment of unions. Dr. F. R. Leavis, in *The Great Tradition* (1948), found it

> of all Dickens's works . . . the one that has all the strength of its genius, together with a strength no other of them can show—that of a completely serious work of art. . . . in *Hard Times* he is for once possessed by a comprehensive vision, one in which the inhumanities of Victorian civilisation are seen as fostered and sanctioned by a hard philosophy, the aggressive formulation of an inhumane spirit.

This valuation was for a while influential, but as Leavis's reputation has declined, *Hard Times* is increasingly seen as one of a group of 'condition of England' novels, together with Disraeli's *Sybil* (1845), Charles Kingsley's *Yeast* (1848) and *Alton Locke* (1850), and Mrs. Gaskell's masterly *North and South* (1855). Louis Cazamian wrote a useful study in 1903 entitled *Le Roman Social en Angleterre*. A translation by Martin

Fido was published in 1973 under the title of *The Social Novel in England 1830–1850*.

Little Dorrit (1855–57) was considered by George Bernard Shaw to be Dickens's masterpiece; it is undoubtedly one of his most powerful novels. It has an autobiographical element, in that Little Dorrit's father, William Dorrit, spends twenty-three years in the Marshalsea debtors' prison, an experience which destroys him psychologically, so that he lives a life of pretence. Mr. Dorrit gives himself pathetic airs of affected dignity. His daughter Amy, Little Dorrit, who remains uncorrupted, grieves at her father's pretence that his degradation is not real—this pretence is the biggest degradation of all. Amy has a selfish, snobbish sister Fanny, and a feckless brother, Tip. She alone contributes to the family's keep, by working as a sempstress in the crumbling house of the paralysed Mrs. Clennam. The main story, a study of the psychological effects of long confinement, is masterly. *Little Dorrit* is sombre, but gripping and moving. It opens in a Mediterranean prison, which seems totally unconnected with the main narrative, until the end, when the two are not very convincingly connected. But Arthur Clenman's home is also a prison; Dickens attacks the rigidity of joyless and repressive religion which blighted the lives of so many Victorian children. That Dickens's own children in the main disappointed him does not vitiate his post-romantic concern for the natural development of the child's capacities.

A Tale of Two Cities, though popular, is inferior work. Dickens's imagination is here working at second-hand, the materials being Thomas Carlyle's *The French Revolution*.

His next full-length novel was the brilliant *Great Expectations* (1860). This is another story of a displaced and unhappy child, harshly brought up 'by hand'. (Incidentally, the American journal *Nineteenth Century Fiction* had a learned article about the meaning of this phrase, obvious to anybody who has had anything to do with the rearing of lambs: it means bottle-fed, instead of on mother's milk.) *Great Expectations* is uniquely satisfying among Dickens's novels: there is no strain in the plotting, and the characters are unforgettable. Miss Havisham is a study of a woman traumatized by shock; grotesquely, she perpetually wears the wedding gown in which she was jilted, keeps the clocks permanently fixed at the time it happened, and her wedding cake, 'like a black fungus', lies rotting on the table, with 'speckle-legged spiders with blotchy bodies running home to it'. This neglect parallels her emotional death and decay. She looks to Pip like a fairy godmother, but she turns out to be the malevolent fairy. Estella is a sleeping beauty, and it is improbable that she would ever overcome the effects of such a crippling childhood. *Great Expectations* is the moral fable of social mobility: the cost is always stress on the primary relationships; to outgrow one's background is expensive. Bernard Shaw commented: 'The reappearance of Mr. Dickens in the character of a blacksmith's boy may be regarded as an apology to Mealy Potatoes', one of his companions in the blacking warehouse. Angus Calder describes the fable as 'a kind of inverted Cinderella, where the ugly sisters, Joe and Magwitch, are in the right. . .'. He also points out that Pip actively helps Miss Havisham and Magwitch to become better people at the end of their lives, thus becoming a true gentleman. I quote from Calder's Introduction to the Penguin English Library edition.

When *Our Mutual Friend* appeared in 1864–65, Henry James accused Dickens of 'wanting in inspiration'; the novel was 'forced'. But Henry James was not a generous reviewer to rivals. The plot is complex, but coherent, a picture of society at the extremes of poverty and wealth: the source of that wealth is 'dustheaps', or human manure. And the novel offers a rich gallery of grotesques. Far from being exhausted, Dickens's invention was at its most fertile in this penultimate novel, about muck and brass and what Thomas Carlyle (whose vision of Victorian England influenced all the 'condition of England' novelists) called 'the cash nexus'. Dickens's prose style was his own invention, but nevertheless reflected the rhetoric of Carlyle, especially in *Past and Present* (1843).

While the earlier view of Dickens as social reformer has been weakened by historians who point out that most of the evils he attacked belonged to the past when he wrote about them, there is no doubt that Dickens had a powerful social conscience and was an indefatigable worker for charity.

George Orwell commented that

> in several ways *Our Mutual Friend* is a return to the earlier
> manner, and not an unsuccessful return either. Dickens's
> thoughts seem to have come full circle. Once again, individual
> kindliness is the remedy for everything. . . .

Dickens died suddenly, after one of his exhausting reading tours. He left behind an incomplete novel, *The Mystery of Edwin Drood*. Again, far from being exhausted, he
was attempting something new. His friend Wilkie Collins
had published *The Moonstone* in 1868. *The Moonstone* was
a detective story and while *Bleak House* has its Inspector
Bucket, a whole story devoted to a criminal case was a new
departure.

During Dickens's lifetime, he was loved by the broad mass
of the people, but fastidiously rejected by some intellectuals,
who accused him of sentimentality and vulgarity. *The Times*
generally gave him hostile reviews: the paper accused him
of stirring up discontent among the poor. But in the mid-
twentieth century, eighty years after Dickens's death, most
British homes, including working-class ones, had a full set of
Dickens.

7

Charlotte and Emily Brontë

The Brontë story is well-known: the Yorkshire moors round Haworth are haunted not only by the fictional ghosts of Jane Eyre, Heathcliff and Cathy Earnshaw, but by the real-life consumptive daughters of the Rev. Patrick Brontë, who made his way from poverty in Ireland to St. John's College, Cambridge, and the Parsonage at Haworth (now a museum attracting upwards of 200,000 visitors each year). The standard picture of the family is of ingrown original genius, mysteriously flaring up in a Yorkshire village. But their achievement is better understood as the product of an environment of intellectual nourishment, diligent habits of study and the ever-present pressure of poverty. Charlotte's later antagonism towards her alcoholic, drug-addicted epileptic brother, Branwell, was due less to the suppressed incestuous feelings attributed by some commentators than to the fact that while the girls could earn some £16 a year as governesses, Branwell, as a male, could earn £220 by the same work, but was idle. Mrs. Elizabeth Gaskell, novelist friend of Charlotte, wrote the earliest biography. In it she describes the remote village,

> with a background of dun and purple moors, rising and sweeping away yet higher than the church, which is built at the very summit of the long narrow street. All round the horizon there is this same line of sinuous wave-like hills; the scoops into which they fall only revealing other hills beyond, of similar colour and shape, crowned with wild, bleak moors. . . . The flagstones with which [the village street] is paved are placed end-ways, in order to give a better hold to the horses' feet; and, even with this help, they seem to be in constant danger of slipping backwards. The old stone houses are high compared to the width of the street, which makes an

abrupt turn before reaching the more level ground at the head of the village, so that the steep aspect of the place, in one part, is almost like that of a wall. . . .

In her second chapter, Mrs. Gaskell continues to explain:

Even an inhabitant of the neighbouring county of Lancaster is struck by the peculiar force of character which the Yorkshire-men display. This makes them interesting as a race; while, at the same time, as individuals, the remarkable degree of self-sufficiency they possess gives them an air of independence rather apt to repel a stranger. . . . Conscious of the strong sagacity and the dogged power of will which seem almost the birthright of the natives . . . each man relies upon himself. . . . He belongs to that keen, yet short-sighted class, who consider suspicion of all whose honesty is not proved as a sign of wisdom . . . there is little display of any of the amenities of life among this wild, rough population. Their accost is curt; their accent and tone of speech blunt and harsh. . . . They have a quick perception of character, and a keen sense of humour . . . there is much close friendship and faithful service; and for a correct exemplification . . . I need only refer the reader of *Wuthering Heights* to the character of 'Joseph.'

From the same cause come also enduring grudges, in some cases amounting to hatred, which occasionally has been bequeathed from generation to generation. . . .

Such was the material the Brontë sisters drew on when writing their novels. Their mother bore six children in quick succession, and died (probably of cancer). The eldest daughter, Maria, was precociously clever and responsible, taking care of the younger ones: Elizabeth, Charlotte, Branwell, Emily and Anne. During their mother's illness, they learned to be quiet, and would wander, hand in hand, out over the moors. Charlotte was 5 when her mother died, and the household management was taken over by a maternal aunt, Miss Branwell, whom the children respected but did not love. The children were all precocious readers, interested in politics, and collaborated in plays featuring the Duke of Wellington. Miss Branwell taught the girls to sew. A school for the daughters of clergymen, within easy reach of Haworth, offered Mr. Brontë the chance, as he saw it, to educate his girls at a price he could afford. Maria, Elizabeth, Charlotte and Emily all went there. Cowan Bridge, run by the Rev. William Carus-Wilson, was later to become notorious as the original of Lowood School in Charlotte's novel, *Jane Eyre* (1847). Following Dickens's *Nicholas Nickleby*, *Jane Eyre* established the 'dreadful school novel' as a genre. The food at Cowan Bridge was unhygienic, and Maria was very unhappy. Maria was delicate and dreamy, and intellectually advanced for her age. At Cowan Bridge she was punished for being slatternly and her sister Charlotte has memorialized Maria's patient sufferings in *Jane Eyre* in the character of Helen Burns. Maria and Elizabeth died before reaching their teens. Charlotte and Emily were sent back to the school after the deaths of their sisters. Charlotte, aged 9, was now the little mother of the diminished family. Eventually, their father took them away from their school for reasons of health. The removal was fortunate, for there was a new servant at the parsonage, an elderly village woman called Tabitha Aykroyd, known to the children as 'Tabby'. Tabby spoke the local dialect and told the children it 'wur the factories as had driven' the fairies away from the valley. She was strict but kindly. The children received their education from their father, their aunt and Tabby. Emily never mixed with the village people, but put her knowledge of Yorkshire dialect and Yorkshire ways to powerful use in *Wuthering Heights* (1847): that was a great year for English fiction, bringing forth also Thackeray's *Vanity Fair*; Dickens's *Dombey and Son* was appearing in monthly parts, and it was the year of *Jane Eyre*.

The Brontë children produced an enormous quantity of juvenile writing, 'tales, dramas, poems, romances', in Mrs. Gaskell's words, written in a minuscule script imitating print. Charlotte had four styles of handwriting: the eye-straining tiny letters of the juvenilia, a quick and untidy hand for diary jottings, a clear and flowing hand for letters, and a neat formal hand, almost copperplate, the 'best' writing of her essays and fair copies of manuscripts. Emily's handwriting, though less of it survives, is similarly varied. Although the family opinions were Tory, they read both the Tory *Intelligencer* and the Whig *Leeds Mercury*. A fragment left by Charlotte, in 1829, relates that 'Papa bought Branwell some wooden soldiers in

Leeds' and each child adopted one as his own. Charlotte, aged 13, drew up a list of the painters whose works she wished to see: 'Guido Reni, Julio Romano, Titian, Raphael, Michael Angelo, Correggio, Annibal Carraci, Leonardo da Vinci, Fra Bartolomeo, Carlo Cignani, Vandyke, Rubens, Bartolomeo Ramerghi'. As Mrs. Humphry Ward was to point out later, 'there were no children's books at the parsonage', and the children fed voraciously on adult literature. In 1831, when she was 16, Charlotte was sent to school again, to Roe Head. She was a shy, stunted, dowdy, bespectacled girl with an Irish accent picked up from her father. Mary Taylor, who was to become her best friend, told her she was 'very ugly'. Charlotte was very conscious that she had no looks, and her most famous novel has a defiantly plain Cinderella-heroine. Charlotte later said she had been an observer of character since she was 5, and the future novelist soon astonished her schoolmates with her unusual knowledge of literature. She drew easily and knew a great deal about painters and pictures, and was well-informed about politics. She was haunted by the memory of her dead sisters. She was not a hopeful girl and did not expect ever to marry. After two years at the school, she returned home and taught her sisters (Branwell was taught the classics by his father). The brother and sisters remained a self-sufficient unit, walking together on the moors and hardly mixing in the village except to teach in the Sunday school.

When Charlotte was 19, a decision had to be made about Branwell's career. The whole family considered Branwell to be headed for great things: he wrote, drew, was an entertaining talker and was a habitué of the village pub, the Black Bull (still there, two minutes' walk from the house). Branwell has left the best portrait of his three sisters, now in the National Portrait Gallery, London. As Mrs. Gaskell says, Branwell's handling of paint was clumsy, but he was brilliant at catching a likeness. Branwell was sent as a student to the Royal Academy, but came home with nothing to show. Charlotte went as a teacher to her old school and Emily went with her, as a pupil, but Emily could not bear being parted from her home at any time. As Charlotte wrote,

My sister Emily loved the moors. Flowers brighter than the rose bloomed in the blackest of the heath for her;—out of a sullen hollow in a livid hillside, her mind could make an Eden. She found in the bleak solitude many and dear delights; and not the least and best-loved was—liberty. Liberty was the breath of Emily's nostrils; without it she perished. The change from her own home to a school, and from her own very noiseless, very secluded, but unrestricted and unartificial mode of life, to one of disciplined routine (though under the kindest auspices) was what she failed of enduring. Her nature proved here too strong for her fortitude. Every morning, when she woke, the vision of home and moors rushed on her, and darkened and saddened the day that lay before her. Nobody knew what ailed her but me. I knew only too well. In this struggle her health was quickly broken: her white face, attenuated form, and failing strength, threatened rapid decline. I felt in my heart she would die, if she did not go home, and with this conviction obtained her recall. She had only been three months at school; and it was some years before the experiment of sending her from home was again ventured on.

Mrs. Gaskell writes:

This physical suffering on Emily's part when absent from Haworth, after recurring several times under similar circumstances, became at length so much an acknowledged fact, that whichever was obliged to leave home, the sisters decided that Emily must remain there, where alone she could enjoy anything like good health. She left it twice again in her life; once going as teacher to a school in Halifax for six months, and afterwards accompanying Charlotte to Brussels for ten. When at home, she took the principal part of the cooking upon herself, and did all the household ironing; and after Tabby grew old and infirm, it was Emily who made all the bread for the family; and any one passing by the kitchen door, might have seen her studying German out of an open book, propped up before her, as she kneaded the dough; but no study, however interesting, interfered with the goodness of the bread, which was always light and excellent.

Charlotte too failed in health away from home. She withdrew into the world of her imagination, the 'Angria' of her childhood writings in collaboration with Branwell (Emily and Anne's imaginary universe was called Gondal), and suffered depression and panic. She wrote to her friend Ellen Nussey:

> I have some qualities that make me very miserable, some feelings that you can have no participation in—that few, very few, people in the world can at all understand. I don't pride myself on these peculiarities. I strive to conceal and suppress them as much as I can; but they burst out sometimes, and then those who see the explosion despise me, and I hate myself. . . .

Charlotte's writings are full of explosive emotion, bursting out like a volcano. Meanwhile, Emily had gone as a teacher to a school in Halifax. Charlotte reported that Emily did 'hard labour from six in the morning to eleven at night, with only one half-hour of exercise between'.

The daughters of a poor clergyman, the girls were forced to earn their own livings. But there were no professions open to women except the menial work of servants and sempstresses; for educated girls, there was only one career, teaching. Charlotte had fantasies of becoming a professional artist, but her eyesight was too weak. Charlotte wrote a letter to Robert Southey, the poet laureate, sending him a sample of her verse and soliciting encouragement. His reply was crushing:

> The daydreams in which you habitually indulge are likely to induce a distempered state of mind; and in proportion as all the ordinary uses of the world seem to you flat and unprofitable, you will be unfitted for them without becoming fitted for anything else. Literature cannot be the business of a woman's life, and it ought not to be. The more she is engaged in her proper duties, the less leisure will she have for it, even as an accomplishment and a recreation. . . .

Charlotte replied with a self-abasing letter in which she apologized for troubling him; she wrote about her efforts to conform:

> Following my father's advice—who from my childhood has counselled me just in the wise and friendly tone of your letter—I have endeavoured not only attentively to observe all the duties a woman ought to fulfil, but to feel deeply interested in them. I don't always succeed, for sometimes

114

when I'm teaching or sewing I would rather be reading or writing; but I try to deny myself; and my father's approbation amply rewarded me for the privation. Once more allow me to thank you with sincere gratitude. I trust I shall never more feel ambitious to see my name in print. . . .

This shows clearly Charlotte's painful struggle against social pressures and the domination of her father.

Meanwhile, Emily had given up her job and returned home. It was decided she should stay there, while the other three attempted to earn. But Charlotte's health failed again, and in 1840 only Anne was employed. Charlotte and Emily decided to set up a school and issued a prospectus, but no pupils came. Although Emily played the piano with 'precision and brilliancy', the girls lacked that high accomplishment which would qualify them to teach more advanced pupils. Charlotte, back at work as a governess, persuaded Aunt Branwell to lend her and Emily £100 so they could go to Brussels. Her letter says:

Papa will, perhaps, think it a wild and ambitious scheme; but whoever rose in the world without ambition? When he left Ireland to go to Cambridge University, he was as ambitious as I am now. I want us *all* to get on. I know we have talents and I want them to be turned to account. . . .

Charlotte and Emily went to study at Madame Heger's pensionnat, where they studied under the irascible M. Heger. Heger thought Emily cleverer than Charlotte, but Emily did not care much for him or for Brussels. But she made rapid progress in French, German, music and drawing. Charlotte hero-worshipped her married master and fell deeply in love. Heger was a brilliant and exacting teacher. He was so pleased with their progress that Charlotte was employed as English teacher and Emily as music teacher, in exchange for free tuition. The girls returned home when their Aunt Branwell died, leaving everything to them. Branwell, originally the favourite, was left out because of his dissolute life. Charlotte returned to Brussels alone, where she gave English lessons to M. Heger and his brother-in-law. But gradually she grew lonely as the observant Madame Heger cooled towards the passionate young Englishwoman. Mrs.

Gaskell, who knew the full story but wished to protect Charlotte's reputation and doubtless that of the Hegers, still alive, put this coolness down to conflict between Madame Heger's Catholicism and Charlotte's Protestantism, inherited from her Ulster father. Similarly, Mrs. Gaskell attributed Charlotte's despair after her return not to unrequited love but to anxiety over Branwell. In 1845, Charlotte found some poems in Emily's handwriting and realized her sister was a true poet. Emily was furious at the intrusion. She was a solitary, self-sufficient person and Charlotte was possibly afraid of her fierceness. Anne then brought out some poems and Charlotte arranged to have all their poems published under the pseudonyms of Currer, Ellis and Acton Bell (names deliberately ambiguous as to gender). The poems were published at their own expense and two copies were sold. Branwell continued to drink and to make everybody miserable, refusing to work. A reviewer spotted that Ellis Bell's poems were better than those of 'his brothers'. Mr. Brontë had an operation for cataract. The girls were trying to persuade Aylott and Jones, publishers of their poems, to take on novels. At nine o'clock every night they would walk up and down the sitting room, reading their work aloud to each other. Charlotte, at 30, complained that her youth had gone like a dream, and she had done nothing. *Jane Eyre* was progressing, *The Professor* was rejected again and again, but Emily's *Wuthering Heights* and Anne's *Agnes Grey* had been accepted, but remained unpublished. *Jane Eyre* came out six weeks after it arrived at the publisher's and caused a sensation. After reading it, her father said, 'Girls, do you know Charlotte has been writing a book, and it is much better than likely?' *Jane Eyre* was dedicated to Thackeray, which caused gossip, as Thackeray, like Mr. Rochester, had a mad wife. People said the author of *Jane Eyre* must be a cast-off mistress of Thackeray.

Charlotte wrote to G. H. Lewes:

> Why do you like Miss Austen so very much? I am puzzled on that point. What induced you to say that you would rather have written *Pride and Prejudice*, or *Tom Jones*, than any of the Waverley Novels?
>
> I had not seen *Pride and Prejudice* till I read that sentence of

yours, and then I got the book. And what did I find? An accurate, daguerrotyped portrait of a commonplace face! a carefully-fenced, highly-cultivated garden, with neat borders and delicate flowers; but no glance of a bright, vivid physiognomy, no open country, no fresh air, no blue hill, no bonny beck. I should hardly like to live with her ladies and gentlemen, in their elegant but confined houses. . . .

Meanwhile, the authorship of the novel was a secret. *Jane Eyre* was successful in America, where it was believed that *Jane Eyre, Wuthering Heights* and Anne's *The Tenant of Wildfell Hall* were all written by the same person. Charlotte and Anne went to London by train and presented themselves, two slim young women dressed in black. The publisher, Mr. George Smith, took them, in their provincial clothes, to the opera.

Branwell died, his promise unfulfilled, his death a relief to all but his shattered father. Emily grew ill and never went out of doors again. Charlotte wrote:

> Stronger than a man, simpler than a child, her nature stood alone . . . while full of ruth for others, on herself she had no pity; the spirit was inexorable to the flesh; from the trembling hands, the unnerved limbs, the fading eyes, the same service was exacted as they had rendered in health.

Emily, breathless and emaciated, refused to see a doctor, until the last, when it was too late. She died a couple of months after her brother. Mrs. Gaskell writes:

> As the old, bereaved father and his two surviving children followed the coffin to the grave, they were joined by Keeper, Emily's fierce, faithful bull-dog. He walked alongside of the mourners, and into the church, and stayed quietly there all the time that the burial service was being read. When he came home, he lay down at Emily's chamber door, and howled pitifully for many days. Anne Brontë drooped and sickened more rapidly from that time. . . .

Anne was convinced she might get better if she could only get to Scarborough. But she died and was buried there. Charlotte wrote to her friend Ellen Nussey,

> To sit in a lonely room—the clock ticking loud through a still house—and have open before the mind's eye the record of the last year, with its shocks, sufferings, losses—is a trial.

Charlotte had already begun the novel, *Shirley*, which had to be finished without the support of her sister-novelists. *Shirley* is very much a Yorkshire novel, and suspicion of its authorship leaked out. Charlotte waited in vain for replies to her letters to M. Heger. She visited Thackeray and Harriet Martineau. Painfully shy, she suffered from headaches and anxiety in company, though she made a good impression on those she met. She was taken up by Sir James and Lady Kay-Shuttleworth; medical man, politician and educationist, Sir James was an important man. He invited Charlotte to London, visiting friends and relatives on the way. But Charlotte refused, because her father was poorly. The social whirl would have been to Charlotte 'like red hot plough-shares', but she was sorry to miss her seat in the ladies' gallery of the Royal Literary Fund Society dinner at Freemason's Hall, where she could have peered down on Thackeray, Dickens and others. She visited Scotland with George Smith.

Wuthering Heights and Anne's *Agnes Grey* were republished, edited with a preface by Charlotte. She decided to

> modify the orthography of the old servant Joseph's speeches; for though, as it stands, it exactly renders the Yorkshire dialect to a Yorkshire ear, yet, I am sure Southerns must find it unintelligible; and thus one of the most graphic characters in the book is lost on them.

This was unnecessary, as Emily's rendering of Yorkshire speech is perfectly clear and wonderfully vivid—but apart from Maria Edgworth's novels half a century earlier, the regional novel, with local dialect, had not been invented. Charlotte found the work depressing: 'the deadly silence, solitude, desolation, were awful; the craving for companionship' plagued her. Struggling on alone, she finished *Villette*, based on her Brussels experience, now ten years old. Her early version, *The Professor*, was steadily refused by her publisher during her lifetime.

For seven years, her father's curate, Arthur Nicholls, had loved Charlotte. It was he who had self-effacingly made himself useful walking the dogs when Emily and Anne were too ill to go out. When Charlotte published *Shirley*, in which he figured as 'Mr. Malone', he gave her a tactful present: it was a leather-bound prayer-book, inscribed in Charlotte's delicate penmanship, 'Charlotte Brontë, Haworth. Presented by Mr. Nicholls on the publication of "Shirley".' I had the luck to discover it in the manuscript collection of the University Library, Cambridge, where it had lain, unknown to Brontë scholars, since 1923, when it had been bought by the then librarian. Mr. Nicholls was the fourth man to propose marriage to Miss Brontë, but she rejected him. He decided to emigrate to Australia. After saying goodbye, Charlotte found him sobbing in the lane. Mr. Nicholls was replaced by a less conscientious curate, and Charlotte was secretly in contact with Mr. Nicholls, who had not gone abroad after all. Mr. Brontë was furious at the idea of his brilliant daughter throwing herself away on a mere country curate: the veins stood out on his neck like whipcord. Charlotte's sympathiès veered towards Mr. Nicholls, and they became engaged. She was not in love, but she liked and respected him, though she wrote sadly to a friend, 'Mr. Nicholls is not intellectual' and their religious views were not identical. It was agreed the couple would live with Mr. Brontë. Charlotte was grateful for his love for her, and hoped she would be able to love him back. She respected his principles. Mr. Brontë could not bring himself to go to the wedding, and Charlotte was given away by her old schoolmistress, Miss Wooler. The honeymoon was spent in Ireland, and Charlotte was agreeably surprised to find her in-laws did not live in cabins as her father had done, but were educated professional people.

Gradually Charlotte grew to love her kind husband, but although theoretically he encouraged her writing, he kept her busy with the duties of a clergyman's wife, such as organizing parish teas. She caught a cold after a walk to see a waterfall and fell ill, unable to keep down any food. She was believed to be pregnant. She died before reaching the age of 40, after nine months of married life. Mr. Nicholls stayed with Mr. Brontë until the old man died, then he returned to Ireland, taking Charlotte's memorabilia with him, wrapped in brown paper.

Jane Eyre made a sensation and continues the most popular of the Brontë novels. The plot concerns an orphan girl reared

by a harsh aunt who has three children of her own. The
orphan is unhappy and, under ill-treatment, turns rebel-
lious. She is punished and sent away to a terrible boarding
school, where she makes a friend, Helen Burns. Helen is
also unjustly punished for her dreamy ways, her superior
intellect unrecognized. Consumptive Helen dies, rejecting
the school's grim religious teaching and having formulated a
more tolerant creed of her own (for further analysis, see my
Charlotte Brontë: Truculent Spirit (Vision Press, 1987)). Helen
Burns is a portrait of Charlotte's sister Maria, who haunted
Charlotte's dreams for many years. The headmistress, Miss
Temple, shows kindness both to Helen and Jane, defying
the harsh Evangelical clergyman, Mr. Brocklehurst, who
enjoins humility on the charity children, while his own
wife and daughters flaunt silk and feathers. After sickness
kills several pupils, the school management is reformed, and
Jane benefits from her education. Grown up, she answers an
advertisement for a governess in Yorkshire. She finds a large
gloomy mansion and a small French girl, Adèle Varens. The
master of the house is Edward Rochester, twice Jane's age, an
embittered roué. He sets out to tease and provoke her, and
Jane stands up for herself. Gradually she falls in love with
him, and suffers bitter jealousy when he entertains County
friends while she is just the governess. There are mysterious
goings-on—a fire in the night, a stabbing—but Jane realizes
her master needs sympathy. They become engaged, but
the engagement is marred by Mr. Rochester's intention of
turning his plain, Quakerish governess into a flaunter of his
wealth, in fine clothes and jewels. Jane wins the contest,
refusing to acquiesce in his sultan-like behaviour, and accepts
two dresses, one grey, one black. The night before the wedding an apparition enters Jane's room and tears her wedding
veil in two. The pieces are on the floor in the morning. The
wedding ceremony is interrupted by a London solicitor and
Richard Mason, who declare an impediment: Mr. Rochester
is already married to Richard's sister, Bertha, the lunatic who
has been setting fires and attacking with knives. Shattered,
Rochester pleads with Jane to become his mistress, but she
runs away. She is taken in by a clergyman, St. John Rivers,
and his sisters Diana and Mary. She recovers and becomes

a teacher at the local school. Jane has assumed the name of Elliott, but in a careless moment lets slip her true identity. The Rivers family who have adopted her are cousins; Jane is heiress to a fortune, which she divides into four. Her cousin St. John is in love with Rosamond Oliver, but considers love an unworthy distraction. He pressures Jane to marry him and go with him to India as a missionary, and Jane is tempted, when she hears Rochester's voice calling her. She leaves St. John and returns to Thornfield, to find a blackened ruin. Rochester is living at Ferndean, a damp and unhealthy spot, maimed and blinded. He has tried to save the life of mad Bertha in the flames, but her brains are dashed out. Jane and Rochester are tenderly reunited and married.

This plot is familiar in outline to people who have never read *Jane Eyre*; it recapitulates Richardson's *Pamela* in that it is about a servant who marries her master. The plot whereby a girl goes as governess or secretary to a gloomy mansion with an employer who seems harsh and remote, but turns out to be a passionate lover (sometimes wounded by fate), is a staple of cheap fiction. (Among the more successful variations on the theme is Daphne du Maurier's *Rebecca*, a truly subversive novel in that the heroine condones her husband's murder of his first wife. Dramatized versions of *Rebecca* always cheat this dénouement out of existence.) Charlotte also took a trick from Scott's *Ivanhoe*, where the madwoman Ulrica falls screaming from a burning castle to her death. The mixture is heady: contemporaries were shocked by the heroine's impetuosity in falling in love before the man had declared his love for her; by the revelations Mr. Rochester makes to Jane about his mistresses, including Adèle's mother, though he disclaims paternity; by the violence of the action and the language. Defenders of Cowan Bridge school claimed that the Rev. Carus Wilson had been unfairly treated in the book. In *Jane Eyre* Charlotte poured out her two great longings—for love and for financial independence. The first has attracted much comment, the second has been often read as evidence of the author's maladjustment. Feminist readings, though often skewed, have been juster to Charlotte than were her contemporaries.

Charlotte's prose is powerful and vivid, her narrative swift. It is a novel of transmuted autobiography and of wish-fulfilment, but nonetheless memorable for that. *Jane Eyre* is full of the language of physiognomy: Jane writes of having 'an organ of veneration', in accordance with the theory that character could be read by the bumps on the skull. Such period eccentricities, however, have not stopped the story being a favourite world-wide. It is especially loved in China and Japan.

Charlotte's next novel, *Shirley*, appeared in 1849. It takes its place among the 'industrial novels' of the '40s. The social conscience of the middle-class public was stirred by the miseries of factory life. Rural squalor had been accepted as a fact of life, but industrial squalor, the product of change, aroused concern. This concern was largely stimulated by Thomas Carlyle in *Chartism* (1839) and *Past and Present* (1843). Carlyle attacked the 'mechanical age', yet found paradoxical grandeur in Manchester's machinery. He pleaded for 'baths, air, a wholesome temperature, ceilings twenty feet high' in factories. His message was that *laissez-faire* policies, combined with social neglect of the poor in industrial areas where there were no squires or clergymen to lead, were driving the ranks of society further apart and could easily foment revolution. His metaphors were apocalyptic: abysses, crumbling cliffs, falls through glass on to spiked iron railings, horses galloping out of control. Disraeli had published *Coningsby* (1844) and *Sybil* (1845), advocating social welfare plus a firm hand; Dickens in *Dombey and Son* and Mrs. Gaskell in *Mary Barton*, both of which had appeared in 1848, demanded from the manufacturers a change of heart. Charlotte's novel suggests paternalism as a solution—leadership plus social welfare. Chartism had just failed, although five of its 'six points' of demand are now taken for granted: equal electoral areas, universal suffrage, payment of Members of Parliament, no property qualification, vote by ballot and annual Parliaments. The Reform Bill of 1832 had enfranchised only the middle class, and Chartists were seen as dangerous agitators. *Shirley* is only incidentally an 'industrial novel', and the main focus of interest has been found in its analysis of female unemployment and financial dependence, and the inadequacy of the clergy. It was produced in terrible conditions: Charlotte wrote to W. S. Williams, her publisher's reader,

> Lonely as I am, how should I be if Providence had never given me courage to adopt a career—perseverance to plead through two long weary years with publishers till they admitted me? How should I be with youth past, sisters lost, a resident in a moorland parish where there is not a single educated family?

Sensitive to attacks on the 'melodrama' of *Jane Eyre*, Charlotte set out to write a novel 'as unromantic as Monday morning'. The Chartist petition was too recent, so the novel is set back to the beginning of the century, the time of the Luddite riots. The wool industry at that time was in recession, and workers resisted the introduction of machinery. The mill-owner, Robert Gérard Moore, installs new machinery, which puts men out of work. The men retaliate by attempting to destroy his mill and kill him. He asks the rich local heiress Shirley Keeldar to marry him, but she indignantly rejects him, as she is in love with his brother Louis. In accordance with Charlotte's preoccupations, the brothers are half-Belgian. Louis is Shirley's tutor.

The real focus of our interest is Caroline Helstone, who is in love with Robert. Caroline is an orphan, with neither money nor occupation. Her uncle, a selfish, hidebound Tory clergyman, dismisses her request to earn a living.

In Chapter 12 we find a key passage:

> 'Caroline,' demanded Miss Keeldar abruptly, 'don't you wish you had a profession—a trade?'
>
> 'I wish it fifty times a day . . . I long to have something absorbing and compulsory to fill my head and hands, and to occupy my thoughts.'

Caroline's thoughts are torture, since she is pining with unrequited love. She tries to tire herself with long walks in all weathers, but remains sleepless, writing letters to Robert which she does not send; she forces herself to do good works for the benefit of the poor. Caroline's misery demonstrates the emptiness of the Victorian recipe for single women—to find satisfaction in being useful. And what heals Caroline when she falls ill is the restorative love of her rediscovered mother. Marriage to Robert comes later. Her social position makes useful, lucrative employment impossible, so she is condemned to genteel poverty. If the lot of the spinster is poverty and indignity, the novel shows that marriage does not necessarily bring happiness. Caroline's long-lost mother, Mrs. Pryor, has had a nightmare marriage to a drunken, violent man, and has given away her daughter. Mrs. Yorke, the mother of Caroline's friend, Rose, is married and mother of a large family, but she is neither happy, nor fulfilled, nor loved by her children. Yet old maids are universally sneered at.

Even the independent Shirley succumbs at last. Shirley is lady of the manor, beautiful and dressed in expensive silks. She has a fierce dog, Tartar. Charlotte told Mrs. Gaskell that Shirley is what Emily Brontë might have been, 'had she been placed in health and prosperity', but this puzzled Mrs. Gaskell, who never met Emily and did not find what she knew of her appealing. Shirley lacks 'the harshness of her peculiar character', despite having a fierce dog and the unfeminine habit of whistling. Shirley is determined to defend her property, but believes it to be her moral responsibility to help the unemployed poor (the standard humane Victorian compromise). It is Shirley who helps Robert with a loan, so that Robert can afford to invest in his business and to marry. Meanwhile, the economy has picked up.

Shirley is a more political novel than is generally recognized: the Tory clergyman, Mr. Helstone, and the radical Mr. Yorke, are fully grasped. And the viewpoint of the workmen is put by Joe Scott, who speaks a wonderfully salty Yorkshire dialect.

In *Villette*, her last novel (1853), Lucy Snowe goes to Belgium to teach in a school run by the cool, capable, unscrupulous Madame Beck (Madame Heger, after the book's publication, recognized herself and refused to be interviewed by Mrs. Gaskell). However, in the novel Madame Beck is not the happy mother of a family as was Madame Heger, but a scheming widow, and the Monsieur-Heger-figure, Monsieur Paul Emanuel, is her bachelor cousin. Lucy is originally half in love with the school's English doctor, the handsome John Bretton, but she realizes she does not appeal to him as does the shallow and flirtatious Ginevra Fanshawe. Eventually John marries Paulina, who adored him when she was a little girl. The waspish Paul Emanuel originally annoys Lucy, but they come to love each other, after they have defied the triple-headed Catholic junta of Père Silas, Madame Beck and the grotesque Madame Walravens, grandmother of Paul's dead love, now living on his charity, bedecked with jewels like a barbarian queen. Paul leaves on a long journey across the ocean, leaving Lucy in possession of her own school which he has rented for her. But storms intervene—'the Atlantic was strewn with wrecks'—and though Mr. Brontë is said to have pleaded with Charlotte for a happy ending, the idea of death at sea was fixed in Charlotte's mind. As she wrote to her publisher, 'Drowning and matrimony are the fearful alternatives.'

Villette has been preferred by many critics to *Jane Eyre*. Like *Jane Eyre*, it has a plain heroine, but Lucy is, in Charlotte's own words, 'morbid and weak at times'. Lucy, like Charlotte, makes a confession in a Catholic church, but fails to go back for instruction by the priest. Charlotte's anti-Catholicism was, all her life, virulent. Lucy's unsuccessful struggle is to repress emotion and the 'heated and discursive imagination', as her unattractive exterior and her social situation demand: *Villette* is a painfully ironic account of the price of frustration, socially imposed and unsuccessfully internalized. *Villette* is even more possessed with death than was *Jane Eyre*, with its invocation of the River Styx, its howling banshee winds and storms. In *Jane Eyre* Rochester is punished for his domineering masculinity; in *Villette*, Charlotte punishes her first-person narrator, Lucy, for everything Charlotte most disliked in herself. Charlotte hesitated whether to call her heroine 'Miss Frost' or 'Miss Snowe'. The novel ponders the problem of those who deserve love and get it, like Paulina; those who do not deserve love, but get it all the same, like Ginevra; those who neither deserve love nor get it, like Madame Beck, who wishes to marry Paul; and Lucy, who is unsure whether or not she deserves love, but gets it just the same. But like that of Lucy's first employer, Miss Marchmont, her happiness is brief, snatched away by the premature death of the loved one.

Quite a lot is known about Charlotte, from her letters and from people who knew her. Emily is more of a mystery:

reclusive, she died before she was 30, with only one novel and a few poems in print. She received small praise for one of the greatest among great English novels. A critique of *Jane Eyre* in the *North American Review*, October 1848, said:

> When the admirable Mr. Rochester appears, and the profanity, brutality and slang of the misanthropic profligate give their torpedo shocks to the nervous system . . . we are gallant enough to detect the hand of a gentleman in the composition. There are also scenes of passion, so hot, so emphatic, and condensed in expression, and so sternly masculine in feeling, that we are almost sure we observe the mind of the author of *Wuthering Heights* at work in the text.

Charlotte read this review aloud to her dying sister, and described the scene to Mr. Williams: Ellis, the 'man of uncommon talents, but dogged, brutal and morose', sat

> . . . looking, alas! piteously pale and wasted; it is not his wont to laugh, but he smiled half-amused and half in anger as he listened. Acton was sewing, no emotion ever stirs him to loquacity, so he only smiled too. . . . How I laugh in my sleeve when I read the solemn assertions that *Jane Eyre* was written in partnership, and that it 'bears the marks of more than one mind and more than one sex'.

Charlotte told Mrs. Gaskell that all Emily's love went towards animals. She writes:

> The helplessness of an animal was its passport to Charlotte's heart; the fierce, wild intractability of its nature was what often recommended it to Emily. Speaking of her dead sister, the former told me that from her many traits in Shirley's character were taken; her way of sitting on the rug reading, with her arm round her rough bull-dog's neck; her calling to a strange dog, running past, with hanging head and lolling tongue, to give it a merciful draught of water, its maddened snap at her, her nobly stern presence of mind, going right into the kitchen, and taking up one of Tabby's red-hot Italian irons to sear the bitten place, and telling no one, till the danger was well-nigh over, for fear of the terrors that might beset their weaker minds. All this, looked upon as a well-invented fiction in *Shirley*, was written down by Charlotte with streaming eyes; it was the literal true account of what Emily had done. The same tawny bull-dog (with his 'strangled whistle'), called

'Tartar' in *Shirley*, was 'Keeper' in Haworth parsonage; a gift to Emily. With the gift came a warning. Keeper was faithful to the depths of his nature as long as he was with friends; but he who struck him with a stick or whip, roused the relentless nature of the brute, who flew at his throat forthwith, and held him there till one or the other was at the point of death. Now Keeper's household fault was this. He loved to steal upstairs and stretch his square, tawny limbs, on the comfortable beds, covered over with delicate white counterpanes. But the cleanliness of the parsonage arrangements was perfect; and this habit of Keeper's was so objectionable, that Emily, in reply to Tabby's remonstrances, declared that, if he was found again transgressing, she herself, in defiance of warning and his well-known ferocity of nature, would beat him so severely that he would never offend again. In the gathering dusk of an autumn evening, Tabby came, half triumphant, half trembling, but in great wrath, to tell Emily that Keeper was lying on the best bed, in drowsy voluptuousness. Charlotte saw Emily's whitening face and set mouth, but dared not speak to interfere; no one dared when Emily's eyes glowed in that manner out of the paleness of her face, and when her lips were so compressed into stone. She went upstairs, and Tabby and Charlotte stood in the gloomy passage below, full of the dark shadows of coming night. Downstairs came Emily, dragging after her the unwilling Keeper, his hind legs set in a heavy attitude of resistance, held by the 'scruff of his neck', but growling low and savagely all the time. The watchers would fain have spoken, but durst not, for fear of taking off Emily's attention, and causing her to avert her head for a moment from the enraged brute. She let him go, planted in a dark corner at the bottom of the stairs; no time was there to fetch stick or rod, for fear of the strangling clutch at her throat—her bare clenched fist struck against his red fierce eyes, before he had time to make his spring, and, in the language of the turf, she 'punished him' till his eyes were swelled up and the half-blind, stupefied beast was led to his accustomed lair, to have his swelled head fomented and cared for by the very Emily herself. The generous dog owed her no grudge; he loved her dearly ever after. . . .

Emily was tall and ungainly, and insisted on wearing out-of-date clothes (probably for economy's sake). Mrs. Gaskell describes her skirts as hanging 'straight and long, clinging to her lank figure'. Her reserve made her unpopular in Belgium, though Charlotte's friend Ellen Nussey was fond of her. Emily's father taught her to shoot. According to the stationer John Greenwood, when practising she would give the pistol back to her father, saying 'load again, papa' and then go back to

> the kitchen, roll another shelf-full of teacakes, then wiping her hands, she would return again to the garden and call out, 'I'm ready again, papa', and so they would go on until he thought she had had enough practice for that day.

Emily, unlike her sisters, never taught in the village Sunday school. Emily regarded religion as a private matter between herself and her God. Her poems describe mystic experience. Her religious faith was strong, but hardly orthodox. Her poem, 'No Coward Soul is Mine', goes:

> No coward soul is mine
> No trembler in the world's storm-troubled sphere
> I see Heaven's glories shine
> And Faith shines equal arming me from Fear.
>
> O God within my breast,
> Almighty ever-present Deity,
> Life that in me has rest
> As I Undying Life, have power in thee.
>
> Vain are the thousand creeds
> That move men's hearts, unutterably vain,
> Worthless as withered weeds
> Or idlest froth amid the boundless main
>
> To waken doubt in one
> Holding so fast by thy infinity
> So surely anchored on
> The steadfast rock of Immortality. . . .

Ellen Nussey remembers Emily with her hand in a moorland rockpool, moralizing on the sticklebacks, on the strong and the weak, the brave and the cowardly. Emily's chief characteristics seem to have been her courage and her self-sufficiency. Yet the picture of her as eccentric and unworldly must be modified in the light of Charlotte's letter to Miss

Wooler mentioning that Emily managed the railway shares the girls had invested in. Emily's biographer, Winifred Gérin, remarks that commentators on *Wuthering Heights* have always rated the legal and financial dealings in the tale to be sound.

The novel is related by a series of narrators, a plan original with Emily Brontë. The first is Lockwood, a timid and conventional southern gentleman, renting Thrushcross Grange. He calls on his landlord, Heathcliff, his only neighbour, and finds a rude welcome and a heap of dead rabbits on a chair. Snowed in, he finds a Testament with the name 'Catherine Earnshaw in it', reads her diary and dreams of her and of hell-fire preaching; dry fir-cones rattle against the window and he knocks his knuckles through the glass and takes hold of 'a little, ice-cold hand'. A voice wails to be let in, and says it is Catherine Linton's. Lockwood tries to get free and rubs the ghostly wrist against the broken glass till blood runs. The voice moans it has been a waif for twenty years. In his nightmare Lockwood has shouted, and Heathcliff comes to complain. Returned home, he asks his housekeeper, Nelly Dean, whose story now takes over, to explain. She relates that Heathcliff was picked up as a waif by old Mr. Earnshaw, father of Catherine and Hindley, in the streets of Liverpool. Catherine loves this adoptive brother dearly, and the pair run wild, but her brother Hindley hates him as a cuckoo in the nest, and after the death of old Mr. Earnshaw persecutes him. Catherine, realizing that if she were to marry Heathcliff, 'we would be beggars', marries the civilized gentleman, Edgar Linton, of Thrushcross Grange. Interrogated by Nelly about her motives, Catherine confesses,

> I've no more business to marry Edgar Linton than I have to be in heaven; and if the wicked man in there had not brought Heathcliff so low, I shouldn't have thought of it. It would degrade me to marry Heathcliff, now; so he shall never know how I love him. . . .

On overhearing that marriage to him would be a degradation, Heathcliff creeps out of the room, before hearing her say:

> My love for Linton is like the foliage in the woods. Time will change it, I'm well aware, as winter changes the trees—my

love for Heathcliff resembles the eternal rocks beneath—a source of little visible delight, but necessary. Nelly, I *am* Heathcliff—he's always in my mind—not as a pleasure, any more than I am always a pleasure to myself—but, as my own being—so, don't talk of our separation again. . . .

Heathcliff returns three years later, having grown rich. He visits Cathy, against her husband's wishes, and to her ecstatic joy. Edgar's sister, Isabella, becomes infatuated with Heathcliff. Catherine warns her this is madness:

Tell her what Heathcliff is—an unreclaimed creature, without refinement—without cultivation; an arid wilderness of furze and whinstone. . . . He's not a rough diamond—a pearl-containing oyster of a rustic; he's a fierce, pitiless, wolfish man. . . . Avarice is growing with him a besetting sin. . . .

Cathy falls ill and resents Edgar's return to his books, 'when I am dying'. Heathcliff elopes with Isabella, whose long letter to Ellen takes over the story. She is, of course, wretched. Heathcliff bursts in on Cathy's deathbed and reproaches her bitterly for desertion. She accuses him of killing her. Catherine gives birth to a daughter, another Cathy, and dies. (The film version, with Laurence Olivier, Merle Oberon and David Niven, was vicious, as it ended here. But like Shakespeare's *The Winter's Tale, Wuthering Heights* is a cyclic tale of regeneration.) Heathcliff then sets about revenging himself on the survivors and acquiring both properties. He brings the widower Hindley, now a drunken wreck, and Hindley's son, Hareton, under his power. Isabella dies and leaves Heathcliff a son, Linton. Heathcliff kidnaps young Catherine, forcing her to marry her cousin, in order to secure the Linton inheritance for himself as well as the Earnshaw property he has appropriated. Nelly gathers information about these events from Zillah, the maid at Wuthering Heights. Heathcliff dies, and young Cathy teaches Hareton to read, thus bringing the young savage into civilization. The novel is about nature and nurture, and the damage done by the denial of love.

Charlotte wrote an editor's preface to a new edition, and noted that southerners

will hardly know what to make of the rough, strong utterance, the harshly manifested passions, the unbridled aversions, and headlong partialities of unlettered moorland hinds and rugged moorland squires, who have grown up untaught and unchecked, except by mentors as harsh as themselves . . . [the novel] is rustic all through. It is moorish, and wild, and knotty as a root of heath . . . she had scarcely more practical knowledge of the peasantry amongst whom she lived, than a nun has of the country people who sometimes pass her convent gates . . . except to go to church or take a walk on the hills, she rarely crossed the threshold of home . . . and yet she knew them: knew their ways, their language, their family histories; she could hear of them with interest, and talk of them with detail, minute, graphic, and accurate; but *with* them, she rarely exchanged a word. Hence . . . what her mind had gathered of the real concerning them, was too exclusively confined to those tragic and terrible traits . . . which, listening to the secret annals of every rude vicinage, the memory is sometimes compelled to receive. . . .

Heathcliff . . . stands unredeemed; never once swerving in his arrow-straight course to perdition, from the time when 'the little black-haired, swarthy thing, as dark as if it came from the Devil', was first unrolled out of the bundle and set on its feet in the farm-house kitchen, to the hour when Nelly Dean found the grim, stalwart corpse laid on its back in the panel-enclosed bed, with wide-gazing eyes that seem 'to sneer at her attempt to close them, and parted lips and sharp white teeth that sneered too' . . . a man's shape animated by demon life—a Ghoul—an Afreet. . . . Whether it is right or advisable to create beings like Heathcliff, I do not know: I scarcely think it is. But . . . the writer who possesses the creative gift owns something of which he is not always master—something that at times strangely wills and works for itself. . . .

Charlotte seems to have been worried by the apparently amoral stance of *Wuthering Heights*, although Heathcliff's violence and cruelty are never justified, despite being understandable and understood. Emily's prose has the clarity, purity and power of the great poet she was.

The shadow of Branwell, of drunkenness, violence and mental instability, haunts the writings of the sisters: in *Jane Eyre* these manifestations occur in Bertha Mason; in *Wuthering Heights* Heathcliff's violence exploits Hindley's drunkenness, and Cathy's attachment to a surrogate brother, an unconsummated passion, may well reflect Emily's grief over Branwell's tragic alienation. Parsonage daughters as they were, the girls had experienced the seamy side of life. It was this that shocked the Victorian public.

8

George Eliot:
The Strong Woman of the
Westminster Review

George Eliot (1819–80) was in every way a remarkable woman: she was immensely learned in literature and the science of her day, reading Greek, Latin, Hebrew, Spanish, Italian and French. Her digested learning gives her novels a uniquely satisfying flavour, so that she has been described as unique in that her novels are 'for grown-up people'. She was born into a lower middle-class family and was spectacularly ugly, so that the young Henry James announced in a letter, 'I have fallen in love with this great horse-faced bluestocking', yet her immensely knowledgeable conversation and her beautifully modulated voice made her company peculiarly charming and sought after. Even her voice was the result of effort: as a child she spoke broad Warwickshire dialect, but when she went to boarding-school she modelled her diction on that of her teachers. She was diffident and self-doubting, suffering headaches and crying fits all her life, yet her achievement was massive.

She was born Mary Anne Evans, later calling herself Mary Ann and eventually Marian, though her nickname was Polly. Her father was a land agent and often drove to the houses of the gentry, his 'little wench' between his knees. The brilliant little girl listened and absorbed the distinctive speech of the different classes she mixed with. Her mother died when she was 16 and she kept house for her father. She had always read widely in theology and German literature. She seems to have had enough money to pay for lessons in the subjects which interested her; she was also a singer and pianist. At school she was very religious, an Evangelical, but she broke away from religion under the influence of Charles Bray, a Coventry ribbon manufacturer. In January 1842 she refused to go to church with her father, which led to a serious breach. In 1843 she went to lodge with Dr. Robert Herbert Brabant, whose intellectual daughter Rufa had married Charles Bray's brother-in-law, Charles Hennell. Brabant was an elderly man whose company delighted her: 'We read and walk and talk together and I am never weary of his company.' The novelist Eliza Lynn Linton, however, thought Dr. Brabant was

> a learned man who used up his literary energies in thought and desire to do rather than in actual doing. . . . Ever writing and rewriting, correcting and destroying, he never got farther than the introductory chapter of a book which he intended to be epoch-making, and the final destroyer of superstition and theological dogma.

Mary Ann had a need to worship. Rufa was working on a translation from the German of David Friedrich Strauss's *Life of Jesus,* which Mary Ann finished and published in 1846. This was a work of the 'higher criticism', a German movement which studied the Bible as literature, concentrating on literary technique and sources. Pioneered by eighteenth- and nineteenth-century German scholars, it grew out of the older textual criticism concerned with the establishment of the best texts. Strauss argued that the Gospels were myth, not fact. Mary Ann said it made her ill 'dissecting the beautiful story of the crucifixion', but she eventually lost all religious faith. However, her work is permeated with the ideals of love, duty and *entsagen* (renunciation). Like many Victorians, she retained Christianity's ethical system after jettisoning its supernatural elements. The publisher of her translation was John Chapman, who lived with a wife and a mistress who was the children's governess. Mary Ann's crush on Dr. Brabant, which had caused gossip, was followed by a crush on Chapman. She moved in as lodger, but the combined jealousy of the other two women drove her out.

At this time she wrote in a letter that Mrs. Hannah More, the Evangelical writer, was that most disagreeable of all monsters, a blue-stocking—a monster that can only exist in a miserably false state of society, in which a woman with but a smattering of learning or philosophy is classed along with singing mice and card-playing pigs.

Distinguished men delighted in Mary Ann's learning. Later, the artist Edward Burne-Jones wrote: 'Her knowledge is really deep, and her heart one of the most sympathetic to me I ever knew.' Her father was dead, and she had to earn a living. Chapman owned a journal, the *Westminster Review*, and Mary Ann became its highly professional commissioning editor. She fell in love with the philosopher Herbert Spencer (1820–1903), who enjoyed her company but was put off by her lack of beauty. One of her contributors was George Henry Lewes, whose wife had given birth to a son by another man. Lewes generously gave the boy his own name, but this meant it was impossible for him ever to be divorced—he had 'condoned' his wife's adultery. In 1853 Mary Ann published a translation of Ludwig Feuerbach's *The Essence of Christianity*, which argued that the myths of Christianity were unnecessary: the good in man was itself divine. This became popularized as a 'religion of humanity', in which Mary Anne concurred. Feuerbach argued that what made a true marriage was love, not legal constraints.

When *Jane Eyre* appeared, Mary Ann wrote to Bray,

> . . . all self-sacrifice is good—but one would like it to be in a somewhat nobler cause than that of a diabolical law which chains a man soul and body to a putrefying carcase.

In 1854 she eloped with Lewes and travelled with him to Germany, where she met Lizst and others, including a princess. Lewes encouraged her to write. A pseudonym was essential. Her social position was equivocal: until she became famous, she was visited hardly at all by respectable women, though old friends were loyal. Her relatives cast her off. She took the name 'George' as a compliment to Lewes. Until he died he cosseted and protected her, though his own health was as fragile as hers and he still took financial responsibility for his wife and her children, kept unfavourable reviews hidden and made it possible for 'Polly' to concentrate. She insisted that she was, in essentials, a married woman and was no longer 'Miss Evans'. Lord Acton commented later that her position was a 'strain' and when 'the hard barrier yielded to her prodigious fame, she received its advance with excessive joy'. She had cast off religion, but believed in Nemesis. Her conversation in the Fellows' garden of Trinity College, Cambridge, is often quoted:

> she, . . . taking as her text the three words which have been used so often as the inspiring trumpet-calls of men—the words, *God, Immortality, Duty,*—pronounced, with terrible earnestness, how inconceivable was the *first*, how unbelievable the *second*, and yet how peremptory and absolute the *third*.

In 1878 Lewes died and she married a friend twenty years younger than herself, John Walter Cross, who edited her *Life and Letters*. Her brother Isaac who had not been in touch for twenty years wrote to congratulate her. Her relations with Cross remain mysterious: he was pulled out of the Grand Canal in Venice on their honeymoon, and his editing of her papers suppressed some materials. She died a few months after her marriage. The standard biography is by Gordon S. Haight, the most penetrating by Ruby Redinger, *George Eliot: The Undiscovered Self*.

Her first published fiction was *Scenes of Clerical Life* (1857). The first and best of these three tales is 'The Sad Fortunes of the Rev. Amos Barton'. Amos is a failure as a priest and as a husband. He does not get on with his parishioners, and is romantically over-impressed with a dubious Countess who sponges on the over-stretched family, taking advantage of sweet Milly Barton's kindness. Milly dies, worn out. Amos is beginning to learn from his misfortune when his incumbency comes to an end and he has to move to a less congenial town parish.

The tender anecdotes about Milly's children revealed, at least to some, the sex of the author, despite the masculine pseudonym. Her next novel, *Adam Bede* (1859), was an instant success. Dinah Morris, the Methodist preacher, is based on memories of George Eliot's Aunt Elizabeth Evans, who told the young girl about spending the night in the condemned cell at Nottingham gaol with a girl who had confessed to murdering her illegitimate child. The story is set back into the eighteenth century. The self-respecting artisan, Adam is, like George Eliot's own father originally, a carpenter by trade. He is in love with Hetty, niece of Martin Poyser. She is pretty but has a 'little butterfly soul'. Mrs. Poyser, the farmer's shrewd wife, with her sharp tongue and homely wisdom, was among the best-loved characters of the period. Hetty is, however, flattered by the admiration of the young squire, Arthur Donnithorne, 'dazzling' to Hetty 'as an Olympian god', who seduces her and of course abandons her. Dinah Morris, calm, serious and self-controlled, does her best to counsel Adam and when Hetty is arrested and tried for infanticide, she does her best to comfort Hetty the night before she is to be executed. Arthur however comes to the rescue with a last-minute reprieve, and Hetty's sentence is commuted to transportation. Adam eventually gets over his grief and marries Dinah, cutting out his brother Seth. Henry James thought this marriage an 'artistic weakness'.

The story follows the seasons and Hetty, despite the author's criticism of her character, is associated with beauty and with fertility: her setting is a grove, a garden; the dairy has coolness and moisture. She looks like a small downy duck or chicken, but Mrs. Poyser says her heart 'is as hard as a pebble'. Hetty lives in Loamshire, the natural 'Eden-like' countryside, whereas Dinah comes from the city, from Stonyshire, where adult suffering is known. Dinah's prayer softens Hetty's heart to repentance.

In this novel George Eliot showed her grasp of country people, their ways and their speech. This was the first novel to introduce working-class people, speaking regional dialect, as main characters. It contains the famous passage:

> I delight in many Dutch paintings, which lofty-minded people despise. I find a source of delicious sympathy in these faithful pictures of a monotonous homely existence, which has been the fate of so many more among my fellow-mortals than a life of pomp or of absolute indigence, of tragic suffering, or of world-stirring actions. I turn without shrinking from cloud-borne angels, from prophets, sibyls and heroic warriors,

to an old woman bending over her flowerpot, or eating her solitary dinner, while the noonday light, softened perhaps by a screen of leaves, falls on her mob-cap, and just touches the rim of her spinning-wheel, and her stone jug, and all those cheap common things which are the precious necessaries of life to her . . . do not impose on us any aesthetic rules which shall banish from the region of Art those old women scraping carrots with their work-worn hands. . . .

She goes on to plead for bonds of sympathy with common, coarse people. She insisted that 'It is needful that you should tolerate, pity and love . . . ugly, stupid and inconsistent people whose movements of goodness you should be able to admire.'

Elsewhere she wrote: 'If art does not enlarge our sympathies, it does nothing morally.'

Queen Victoria admired *Adam Bede* and commissioned two watercolours of scenes from the story by Corbould: one of Dinah preaching, the other of Hetty making butter, watched by Arthur. They are now in Buckingham Palace. The Queen wrote to her eldest daughter: 'There is such knowledge of human nature, and such truth in the characters. . . .'

The Mill on the Floss (1860) has large elements of auto-biography. Passionate, intellectual Maggie Tulliver is constricted by her provincial environment and the failure of her father's business. Maggie worships her brother Tom, who treats her with self-satisfied masculine arrogance and finds her emotional demand intolerable. Mary Ann's own relatives are recalled in the fiercely respectable and thrifty Gleggs, Dodsons, Pullets and Deanes. Maggie's ambition to impress the gipsies with her learning and social position recalls the young Mary Ann Evans who, aged 4, sat down at the piano though she could not play a note and banged away to impress the servant. When the family piano is sold, the only music Maggie gets to hear is in church. Like the young Mary Ann Evans, Maggie becomes religious and attempts self-denial, but her deformed friend Philip Wakem, son of her father's enemy, tells Maggie her adolescent asceticism is merely an attempt to stupefy herself, not to bear sorrow. She has to learn that 'renunciation remains a sorrow, but a sorrow borne willingly.'

Maggie is attracted to her cousin Lucy's young man, Stephen Guest, who wishes to abandon Lucy and marry Maggie. Maggie runs away with Stephen against her conscience and then changes her mind. The author can only make Stephen's reconciliation to Lucy plausible by engineering Maggie's early death: she and her brother are drowned together in a flood.

In 1855 George Eliot wrote an essay on *The Morality of Wilhelm Meister*. In it she expressed her views on 'moralising novelists':

> Just as far from being really moral is the so-called moral dénouement, in which rewards and punishments are distributed according to those notions of justice in which the novel writer should have recommended that the world should be governed if he had been consulted at the creation. The emotion of satisfaction which a reader feels when the villain of the book dies of some hideous disease, or is crushed by a railway train, is not more essentially moral than the satisfaction which used to be felt in whipping culprits at the cart's tail.

The sentiments are high-minded, but in her practice as a novelist she awards her own punishments, always brought on the offender by his own actions: this punishment comes from 'Nemesis', the Greek goddess of retribution, thus excusing the author; in later books, the punishment is exposure, with consequent humiliation.

The germ of *Silas Marner* was a childhood memory of seeing a linen-weaver with a bag on his back. Silas has been driven out of a dissenting community by a false friend who has framed him for theft. He is mildly epileptic and becomes an embittered solitary, caring only for the gold he manages to put aside. The local Squire has two sons, good Godfrey and wicked Dunstan. Godfrey has made a disastrous secret marriage to a drug-addict, Molly. Dunstan blackmails his brother (who is in love with the upright Nancy Lammeter) and steals Marner's gold. Dunstan disappears from the village. Molly, slighted by Godfrey and wishing to be acknowledged, walks in the snow with her child in arms to confront her father-in-law. But she dies on the path, and her daughter Eppie toddles away into Marner's cottage, where he cares for her, tying her to his loom while he works, and growing to love her. She fills the place in his life left vacant by the loss of his gold (love is worth more than money).

The old stone-pit is drained and Dunstan's skeleton and Silas's lost bag of gold are revealed. Godfrey, convinced that 'everything comes to light', confesses to Nancy, now his second wife, that he has been married before and that Eppie is his daughter. Nancy and Godfrey want to adopt her, but she prefers to stick with Silas and to marry Aaron Winthrop, a young man she feels to be of her own class. The novel is another chronicle of rustic manners, a morality and a story of revelation.

The narrative is confident; George Eliot's historical grasp, as well as her homage to Sir Walter Scott, whose works she started reading at 7, is established at the outset:

> In the days when the spinning-wheels hummed busily in the farmhouses—and even great ladies, clothed in silk and thread lace, had their toy spinning-wheels of polished oak—there might be seen in districts far away among the lanes, or deep in the bosom of the hills, certain pallid undersized men, who, by the side of the brawny country-folk, looked like the remnants of a disinherited race. The shepherd's dog barked fiercely when one of these alien-looking men appeared on the upland, dark against the early winter sunset; for what dog likes a figure bent under a heavy bag?—and these pale men rarely stirred abroad without that mysterious burden.

Her next novel was *Romola*, published serially in 1862–63. It is generally accounted a failure, despite the author's prodigious research into the times of Savonarola.

Felix Holt, the Radical appeared in 1866. Like *Silas Marner*, it opens with a wonderful evocation of a vanished past; its period is the Reform Bill of 1832. Felix Holt is an educated man who works as an artisan to keep his mother and to encourage his fellow-workers towards political advance. The plot centres on the local election, in which the wealthy Harold Transome, son of the manor-house, stands for Parliament as a Radical, in opposition to his family's traditional Toryism. There is a riot and Felix, trying to restrain the mob, is unjustly imprisoned. Harold turns out to be the illegitimate son of his father's agent, whom he hates. Felix and Harold compete for the hand of Esther Lyon, who turns out to be the heiress of the Transome estate, and she chooses poverty and true love with Felix.

Middlemarch, a panoramic novel with a double plot, generally considered her masterpiece, appeared serially in 1871–72. The idealistic Dorothea Brooke marries the desiccated pedant, Mr. Casaubon, working on a *Key to All Mythologies,* a characteristic Victorian theoretical enterprise. He never gets anywhere (a reminiscence of Dr. Brabant, though other candidates have been proposed), and Dorothea is disillusioned. On honeymoon in Rome, the Protestant English girl is bewildered by Rome's wealth of art. The second plot concerns Dr. Tertius Lydgate, who marries the beautiful but extravagant and self-willed Rosamond Vincy and gets into debt. Rosamond's brother Fred is in love with Mary, daughter of the admirable estate manager, Caleb Garth (reminiscent of Robert Evans). The rich banker Bulstrode, who has a shady past, is unmasked. Mr. Casaubon has died, but left a will disinheriting Dorothea if she marries his young cousin, Will Ladislaw. Dorothea finds Rosamond and Ladislaw together, but Rosamond with a moment of uncharacteristic generosity which recalls Becky Sharp's revelation to Amelia in *Vanity Fair,* tells Dorothea that Will still loves Dorothea. Dorothea renounces Casaubon's money and marries Will. Fred, disappointed in his expectations of inheriting a fortune, eventually gives up his father's ambitions for him, becomes a land-agent and marries Mary Garth. *Middlemarch* is a rich, wise, analytical novel, with much humour. As a political novel, depicting the Toryism of the Cadwalladers and Chettams, it is sharper than *Felix Holt.*

For some, however, her masterpiece is her last novel, the absorbing *Daniel Deronda* (1876). In it she explores her deepest concerns: egoism, the ties of blood, the nature of professionalism in the arts, and the theme of sacrifice.

Gwendolen Harleth, another spoilt beauty, is first seen in a gambling den. George Eliot had seen Byron's niece, with her fresh young face, in similar circumstances, on the Continent. Gwendolen marries the brutal aristocrat Henleigh Grandcourt, for money, in order to help her mother and sisters. This is against Gwendolen's conscience, for Grandcourt's mistress and mother of his four children, Mrs. Glasher, has been forced to give up the diamonds Grandcourt

gave her to Gwendolen, who rejects Mrs. Glasher's appeals
to leave Grandcourt single. Gwendolen finds she is married
to a cruel, though languid, tyrant. She finds comfort in the
company of the handsome Daniel, apparently an illegitimate
cousin of Grandcourt's, but in fact the son of the Jewish
singer Alcharisi, now a princess, who gave him away at
birth in order to pursue her career, imagining life would be
easier for him if his Jewish birth was concealed. But Daniel
saves a beautiful Jewish girl from drowning and under the
influence of her visionary brother Mordecai becomes interested in Zionism. Grandcourt is drowned in an accident and
Gwendolen fails to throw him a rope. Widowed, she learns
that Daniel is to marry Mirah and devote himself to the Jewish
cause.

A minor character is Herr Klesmer, the Jewish musician
who explains to Gwendolen that her amateurish musician-
ship is nothing like the talent and dedication needed to earn
a living by music. When she says she has heard feeble performances, he retorts: 'That is the easy criticism of the buyer.'
Catherine Arrowpoint, an heiress, gives up her fortune to
marry Klesmer.

The commanding figure of the princess who sends for
her son Daniel when she is dying is a powerful study. The
princess tells Daniel:

> You may try—but you can never imagine what it is to have a
> man's force of genius in you, and yet to suffer the slavery of
> being a girl . . . a woman's heart must be of such a size and no
> larger, else it must be pressed small, like Chinese feet. . . .

The image of bound Chinese feet is economical but powerful, implying crushing, distortion, torture, agony, caused by
the cruel confinement of natural gifts. For the princess, her
talent is a chance to escape from 'bondage'; men like her
father, says the princess, turn their wives and daughters
into slaves. Meeting his mother, Daniel feels as 'if he had
seen her going through some strange rite of a religion which
gave a sacredness to crime'. The princess is punished with
loneliness, a lingering fatal illness, and a pursuing Fury. But
what is her offence? It is often assumed that her crime was
to abandon her religion and give away her son. But it is

arguable that the narrative punished the princess not for her self-assertion as an artist, but for her failure of nerve; she has given up her career:

> I never meant to marry again. I meant to be free, and to live for my art. . . . For nine years I was a queen. . . . But . . . I began to sing out of tune. . . . I could not endure the prospect of failure. . . . I made believe that I preferred being the wife of a Russian noble to being the greatest lyric actress of Europe. . . .

George Eliot was aware of the cost of pursuing her own career. Like the princess, she had cut herself off from her family to follow her destiny. Surely the princess's crime is her refusal to risk failure?

The singer Mirah is sweeter-natured, accepts failure and settles for marriage. Mirah sings music by a fictitious composer Leo. This character is a link with George Eliot's remarkable poem, *Armgart*, published five years earlier. *Armgart* has received only sketchy attention, even from feminist critics. Yet the poem reveals George Eliot's complicated feelings about her womanhood and her artistry, and casts reflected light on Alcharisi. *Armgart* makes it plain that a gifted woman's first duty is to her talent.

Armgart has identified herself with the forces of nature, as a quasi-divinity. Her lover, Dornberg, gives her Mephistophelian advice, counselling her to quit while she is winning: 'A woman's rank lies in the fullness of her womanhood: Therein alone she is royal.'

He insists she must give up her career to marry him. But she becomes ill and loses her voice. She waits for Dornberg to come and claim her, but he has left for India. Without her talent she is just 'a plain brown girl' and of no interest to him. Did George Eliot fear that if she ceased to be a successful writer Lewes would abandon her?

Gordon Haight comments:

> Abandonment by her former suitor Graf Dornberg teaches her that a woman's domestic affections cannot be sacrificed to her artistic life—a theme George Eliot would return to with the Alcharisi in *Daniel Deronda*. . . .

It is surely wilful to conclude that Armgart ought not to sacrifice her affections to her career. In fact, the poem says the opposite: without her talent, the heroine is nothing.

The stories of Alcharisi and Armgart enact George Eliot's worst fears: Armgart is betrayed, losing love when her talent deserts her; Alcharisi betrays her talent by taking the easy way out. Alcharisi ends up emotionally bankrupt, having rejected both father and son, with an aristocratic title but only the memory of her art. Reading *Daniel Deronda* and *Armgart* together, it seems impossible that George Eliot ever thought the gifted woman should settle for domesticity.

Music stands as emblem for the creative arts in *Deronda*. Characters are symbolically named: Herr Klesmer's name comes from Hebrew *klei zemer*, musical instruments. Daniel in the Bible is a judge, and Daniel 'judges' Gwendolen; his friend is Ezra, which means 'help' in Hebrew. The princess's name is Leonora Halm-Eberstein, though her husband is Russian. *'Halm'* is German for blade or knife; she has cut herself off, by baptism, from her Jewish heritage—as George Eliot, embracing agnosticism, cut herself off from her Anglican family. *Eber* means wild boar, while *stein* means a stone. She is savage like a boar, hard like a stone. The figures of Gwendolen and Grandcourt, lifelike as they are, are based on stock characters: the spoilt beauty who is punished for a mercenary marriage, and the brutal aristocrat. The Jewish princess who rejects her father and gives away her baby to become a great artist, but fails and loses everything, is a disturbing and original image.

George Eliot, in rising to greatness, was rejected by her family and chose, deliberately, not to bear children who would be illegitimate. The princess becomes a monster; Mirah, whose talent is not strong enough for success, settles for happy marriage. The princess and Mirah are the first women in English fiction to face the conflict which is a staple of fiction in our own day—marriage or career. This novel, often dismissed as overloaded with Jewish politics, is the climax of George Eliot's work.

9

Thomas Hardy: The Short and Simple Annals of the Poor

Thomas Hardy (1840–1928) followed George Eliot in writing about rural people. Like her, he was a typical Victorian in having lost his early religious faith. Yet both he and she kept the habit of regular Bible-reading, and Hardy all his life kept a faint nostalgia for the devotion of his youth, as expressed in his famous poem, 'The Oxen', in which he recalls being told, as a child, that on Christmas Eve, at twelve midnight, the oxen in the shed habitually knelt in honour of the birth of Jesus Christ. The poem ends:

> So fair a fancy few would weave
>   In these years! Yet I feel,
> If some one said on Christmas Eve,
>   'Come; see the oxen kneel
> 'In the lonely barton by yonder coomb
>   Our childhood used to know',
> I should go with him in the gloom,
>   Hoping it might be so.

However much he hoped it 'might be so', Hardy could not hold on to the comforting belief in Providence. His great novels show human beings engaged in a Darwinian struggle for existence, in a natural world which, if not actively hostile, is indifferent. Contemporaries found this 'pessimism' shocking. Hardy was self-educated and his marvellously eclectic vocabulary has been criticized as eccentric; to some readers, however, his prose has a satisfying grittiness.

Hardy was born in Dorset, the son of a master stonemason. Hardy senior was a skilled musician, a talent inherited by his son, who later joined his father as violinist in the village band which played at church services, weddings and other local occasions. Young Thomas was sent to school and encouraged to read. Between the ages of 10 and 16, he went to a secondary school in Dorchester where he learned mathematics and Latin. He was then apprenticed to an architect, John Hicks, and met the brilliant Horace Moule. The young men used to read Greek together before starting work. Hardy also met the Dorset antiquary and clergyman William Barnes, who wrote poems in local dialect. Hardy as a village boy learned folklore at its everyday level; from Barnes he grasped how to put it in a learned perspective. Hardy was still a regular churchgoer, though the village choirs were giving way to harmoniums, as recorded in his novel *Under the Greenwood Tree* (1872). Darwin's *The Origin of Species* was published in 1859. This work caused a religious upheaval: whereas the Bible had implied Creation, Darwin's theory of evolution argued that life was the result of adaptation to environment; it put into circulation the phrases 'the struggle for existence' and 'the survival of the fittest'. Although Lord Tennyson had recognized at the beginning of the decade that Nature was 'red in tooth and claw' ('In Memoriam'), few contemporaries had taken aboard until Darwin the conflict between the cruelty of Nature and belief in a beneficent providence. One effect of Darwin's book was the development of 'social Darwinism', the idea that poverty and failure were inevitable for the many, and that social injustice was therefore justified. This was an extension of the *laissez-faire* economic theories which defended the worst brutalities of the factory system, and whose problems were addressed in the 'Condition of England' novels. While Hardy certainly did not subscribe to 'social Darwinism', his novels reflect the impact of evolutionary Darwinism. There is a vulgar notion that Hardy's novels show man as puppet in a world dominated by Fate, a gross exaggeration; but they do show, in poignant detail, the impact of creeping industrialization and concomitant social change on traditional agrarian communities and their way of life.

In 1862 Hardy went to work in London for a firm of architects, and stayed five years, taking advantage of the capital's cultural opportunities. Uprooted from the countryside, he lost his religious faith and his health deteriorated. He was, however, writing poems.

He returned to Hicks and in 1871 published his first novel, *Desperate Remedies*. His first important novel was *Far from the Madding Crowd* (1874).

This novel, made into a fine film with Julie Christie and Alan Bates, is about a proud beauty and her faithful lover who wins her in the end. Gabriel Oak is a sheep farmer, but his sheepdog treacherously drives the flock, Gabriel's only capital, over a cliff. He goes to work for the spirited farmer, Bathsheba Everdene, who rides astride like a man, not using the side-saddle more usual for ladies at that time, with whom he is in love. He serves her faithfully, saving the ricks in a storm, curing her sheep of a deadly disease, and is soon promoted from shepherd to bailiff. Bathsheba is captivated by the dashing Sergeant Troy and marries him, after he has failed to marry his pregnant girlfriend, Fanny Robin, a servant of Bathsheba's. (She mistakes the church where they are to be married.) Fanny dies in childbirth. The marriage of Troy and Bathsheba is not happy: he mismanages her farm, squandering her money, and disappears, believed drowned, though he turns up later in a circus. Meanwhile, Bathsheba has frivolously sent her melancholy neighbour, Farmer Boldwood, a Valentine, which precipitates his falling violently in love with her, and he gives a party at which he presses her to marry him. Troy turns up and Boldwood shoots him dead. He is tried and condemned, but his sentence is commuted. Bathsheba eventually recognizes Gabriel's worth and marries him.

Gabriel works with, rather than against, Nature:

> His toe kicked against something which felt soft, leathery and distended, like a boxing glove. It was a large toad, humbly travelling across the path. Oak took it up, thinking it might be better to kill the creature to save it from pain: but finding it uninjured, he placed it again among the grass. He knew what this direct message from the Great Mother meant.

It meant, of course, rain to come. Hardy was the first to write sympathetically about the conditions under which the rural poor and middling people earned their livings.

He wrote to Rider Haggard about Dorset labouring men:

> . . . down to 1850 and 1855 his condition was in general one of the greatest hardship. . . . As a child, I knew by sight a sheep-keeping boy who, to my horror, shortly afterwards died of want, the contents of his stomach at the autopsy being raw turnip only.

Summary and selective quotation cannot do justice to the rich symbolic and mythically allusive texture of his novels. In *Madding Crowd* the slow pace of country life is contrasted with industrial change:

> Five decades hardly modified the cut of a gaiter, the embroidery of a smock-frock, by the breadth of a hair. Ten generations failed to alter the turn of a single phrase.

The success of *Madding Crowd* earned him enough money to marry Emma Lavinia Gifford, whom he had met when surveying a church in Cornwall. Emma's social position was superior to her husband's, and she is generally believed not to have let him forget it. The Hardys lived together in London and in the West Country. His next important novel was *The Return of the Native* (1878). The setting is Egdon Heath, a naturally wild open space. Clym Yeobright returns from life as a jeweller in Paris to his native heath, with the intention of becoming a schoolteacher. His cousin Thomasin Yeobright is married to Damon Wildeve, formerly an engineer, now keeper of a public house. But the marriage is not happy, for Wildeve is in love with the passionate, ambitious Eustacia Vye, and has married Thomasin to spite her. Eustacia, whose head is full of romantic dreams, marries Clym, hoping he will whirl her to Paris and the sophisticated life she imagines he can offer. But Clym's sight fails him, and he is reduced to the humble occupation of cutting furze. There he is surrounded by creeping and winged things which seemed to 'enrol him in their band . . . huge flies, ignorant of larders and quite in a savage state, buzzed about him without knowing that he was a man.'

If the flies know nothing of Clym, Clym knows nothing of Eustacia, 'a pagan goddess', except that she is beautiful; he has failed to recognize that her needs and view of life are incompatible with his, and that she dreams of the 'escape' he has rejected. Eustacia, frustrated, takes up again with Wildeve and in the Mummers' Play she takes the exotic male rôle of the Turkish Knight. Clym and his mother quarrel about Eustacia and Mrs. Yeobright visits the couple, but Eustacia, imagining erroneously that Clym is in the house, does not answer the door. This misunderstanding leads to Mrs. Yeobright trudging back across the heath alone. She is bitten by an adder and dies. Clym and Eustacia quarrel violently and Eustacia leaves home. She and Wildeve are both drowned. Clym, full of grief and remorse, becomes a wandering preacher. Wildeve's widow, Thomasin, returns to her patient, humble lover, Diggory Venn the reddleman, dyed by his trade. 'Ruddle' or 'reddle' is the red dye used to mark sheep.

As always in Hardy, the present drama is played out against a panorama of the past:

> Granfer Cantle and cronies on Rainbarrow supposed they were celebrating something about a Gunpowder Plot, but . . . Festival fires to Thor and Woden had followed on the same ground and duly had their day.

The Mayor of Casterbridge followed in 1886. Michael Henchard gets drunk and sells his wife to a sailor at a country fair. Such cases were common in the nineteenth century and although prosecutions were occasionally brought, as a well-established folk custom wife sales served the purpose of divorces for poor people. A wife would be led to market with a rope round her neck and sold to the highest bidder. Very often, he was her lover. Simple people believed, as does Susan in the novel, that such arrangements had the binding force of law. But in the novel Henchard repents the loss of his wife and also of their daughter, Elizabeth-Jane, to a sailor called Newson. Horrified at what he has done, he takes an oath not to touch liquor again. He becomes a rich grain merchant and Mayor of Casterbridge (Dorchester), a country-town.

Casterbridge was the complement of the rural life around it; not its urban opposite. Bees and butterflies in the cornfields, who desired to get into the meads at the bottom, took no circuitous course, but flew straight down the High Street. . . .

Susan, now widowed, comes back with a daughter, Elizabeth-Jane, to seek Henchard out. Henchard, meanwhile, has become involved with a rich lady from Jersey, Lucetta, but 'marries' Susan. Henchard employs a young Scotsman, Donald Farfrae, as his manager, and eventually Farfrae marries Lucetta and becomes Henchard's successful business rival, with Henchard reduced to working as his labourer. Susan has died and Henchard has learned that his own daughter died; the present Elizabeth-Jane is Newson's child. Henchard treats her harshly. Her real father comes to claim her. Farfrae is now Mayor and after Lucetta dies, as a result of seeing herself and Henchard paraded in effigy, Elizabeth-Jane marries Farfrae. Only she is kind to the outcast Henchard when he falls into degradation and bitterness.

The relationship between Henchard and Farfrae is allusive to that between Saul and David in the Bible. Henchard carries on his business in the old rule of thumb fashion; Farfrae represents the new efficiency, paying lower wages and weighing everything carefully. The novel constantly invokes Britain's past, by revealed Roman artefacts.

Hardy and Emma were not getting on, and *The Woodlanders* (1887) is about the folly of 'rising' to marry out of one's class. Giles Winterbourne, expert in woodland lore, and himself a fertility spirit within the scheme of the novel (his name means 'spring' or 'watersource') is engaged to Grace Melbury, but like Gabriel Oak he has financial difficulties. Grace's father has sent her to finishing school and snobbishly discourages Giles. Melbury wants Grace to catch Dr. Edred Fitzpiers, yet another 'brutal aristocrat' and seducing squire; he has dallied with a local wench, Suke Damson, and Grace is worried about this, but her father pushes her into the match. But Fitzpiers is soon having an affair with the socialite Felice Charmond, whose hair is false. It came from the head of Marty South, who was forced to sell it. It would be hard to find a neater emblem of economic exploitation. Melbury attacks Fitzpiers, who runs away with Mrs. Charmond, who is soon murdered by a former lover. Fitzpiers comes back to England. Grace's father imagines, wrongly, that Grace can divorce her husband (though the law at that time would not have allowed a wife a divorce for adultery without aggravating circumstances). Grace takes shelter at Giles's cottage, and he, to protect her reputation, sleeps outdoors, dying of exposure. Grace and Fitzpiers pick up the tattered threads of their marriage, and Marty is left to mourn Giles: 'But no, no, my love, I never can forget 'ee: for you was a good man, and did good things.' Hardy, writing to a friend, said he liked it '*as a story*, best of all'.

In 1891, *Tess of the D'Urbervilles* was published. Hardy called it the tale of 'a pure woman', but the Victorian public found it hard to accept a heroine who is raped and thus the mother of an illegitimate child. Hardy had seen two hangings before he was 16. One of them was of Martha Brown, who had killed her husband with a hatchet when she found him with another woman on his knee. This other woman walked 25 miles to see her rival's execution, but was finally repulsed by angry villagers. Hardy wrote:

> I remember what a fine figure she showed against the sky as she hung in the misty rain, and how the tight black silk gown set off her shape as she wheeled half-round and back. I hope you have not felt the cold much. . . .

Tess Durbeyfield is the daughter of a poor village family, but she is also, within the story, associated with mythic and historical references, and female pre-Christian cults. Her beliefs are 'Tractarian in phraseology, Pantheistic in essence'. Her father's head is turned when the village clergyman tells him the family is descended from the ancient Norman family of D'Urberville. But Tess has to 'live in the present': Norman blood is not much use, 'unaided by Victorian lucre'. Tess's foolish mother Joan persuades her daughter to make contact with the Stoke-D'Urberville family, not knowing they are *nouveaux-riches* who have assumed the name. She goes to work at their house and is pursued by the son, Alec. Rebuffed, he eventually rapes her: 'there was sobbing in the Chase.'

151

We next see Tess at work in a cornfield, suckling her baby. (The women of the village have a folk custom celebrating Cerealia, the corn goddess, and throughout the novel Tess is associated with fertility goddesses and mother Eve as a child and type of Nature.) Her mother's comment on Tess's loss of virginity is, 'Tis nater, after all, and what do please God!' *Tess*, on one level, is about the opposition of Nature's law and man's. When Tess's child falls ill, she baptises him herself, in the bedroom basin, with the name Sorrow. The child dies, but is refused Christian burial, as a bastard could not then be buried in consecrated ground. The child is buried eventually among the nettles and Tess puts flowers in a marmalade pot on its grave.

She moves to Talbothays Farm as one of four dairymaids. Milk imagery runs through the novel: Tess crosses 'an irregular chalk table land bosomed with semi-globular tumuli: as if Cybele the many breasted were supinely extended there'. She meets Angel Clare, drop-out from a clerical family, with romantic ideas about the 'unspoilt' peasantry. All the girls fall in love with him, but he marries Tess, calling her Artemis (virgin goddess of the moon) and Demeter (corn goddess). They are frequently compared to Adam and Eve. She tries to tell him of her past, but the letter gets stuck underneath the doormat. On their wedding night, Angel confesses to an encounter with a prostitute, and Tess, emboldened, tells her story. Her husband, horrified, rejects her and goes to Brazil. She is reduced to hard fieldwork, and Alec, who has now taken up with religion, reappears, saying she is more his wife than Angel's. Alec is persistently associated with imagery of the devil: he compares her to Eve in Paradise and himself with the tempter, and quotes Milton's poem *Paradise Lost* (1667). He says his 'trap' is waiting to carry her; he means his carriage, but she retorts it is 'the trap you set me'. Alec 'masters' her. Angel, in response to her pleading letters, returns and finds her living with Alec. Tess sends Angel away, and then stabs Alec to death. She runs after her husband and catches him up, saying she has killed Alec 'for the trap he set for me in my simple youth'. They wander on Salisbury Plain and sleep under the Stone of Sacrifice on Stonehenge, where Tess is arrested. Angel Clare and Tess's sister watch while the black flag is raised, a sign that Tess's execution has been carried out.

> 'Justice' was done, and the President of the Immortals, in Aeschylean phrase, had ended his sport with Tess. . . . The two speechless gazers bent themselves down to the earth, as if in prayer, and remained thus a long time, absolutely motionless: the flag continued to wave silently. As soon as they had strength, they arose, joined hands again, and went on.

The reader is reminded of the end of *Paradise Lost*, when Adam and Eve are expelled from Paradise:

> The World was all before them, where to choose
> Thir place of rest, and Providence thir guide:
> They hand in hand with wandring steps and slow,
> Through Eden took thir solitarie way.

Tess is an enthralling story, an original twist on the 'village maiden and wicked squire' plot: indeed, there are two men to take advantage of Tess; both have higher social position. But if Alec has too much of the flesh, Angel is too spiritual, and between them Tess is destroyed. Angel exemplifies bourgeois hypocrisy, while Alec represents the brute power of money—Tess is doubly oppressed, by Victorian morality and by the economic system.

Hardy's next novel, *Jude the Obscure*, was his last. It continued Hardy's meditation on the conflict between flesh and spirit, though here a male character is destroyed by two women, one of whom is too fleshly, the other too spiritual. But readers and reviewers considered it indecent, and Hardy gave up writing fiction. For the next thirty years, he wrote poetry, experimenting continually with stress and verse form. Unlike the work of other writers, his poetry is as distinguished as his fiction.

Jude Fawley is a stonemason, like Hardy's father. Jude dreams of entering the University of 'Christminster' (Oxford), and taking Holy Orders. He studies alone, but is trapped into marriage by the coarse-fibred Arabella, who pretends she is pregnant. Arabella, bored, leaves him. Jude moves into the city and meets his cousin, Sue, sensitive, intellectual and free-thinking. Sue marries Phillotson, a teacher, but leaves him for Jude. Both Sue and Jude are divorced by their partners, but Sue hates the idea of marriage. She bears three children, the eldest of whom murders the other two and hangs himself, 'Done because we are too menny.' Sue, convinced this is divine punishment, goes back to her husband, and Arabella reclaims Jude, who drinks himself to death. Sue's and Jude's opinions were too advanced for their epoch, and the book was condemned as 'grimy', 'dirt, drivel and damnation'; it was burnt by a bishop. Yet it is the most modern of Hardy's novels: in their agnosticism and in their living together unmarried, Sue and Jude prefigure today's world. The intellectual core of the book is the conflict between Hellenism and Hebraism.

I studied the book at Cambridge with Q. D. Leavis, who argued that Jude should have given up his dreams and been satisfied with life as a stonemason. Jude's aspirations were poignant for me, a village girl who had struggled late to university. When I said village life could not satisfy Jude's intellect, she assured me the 'organic community' was productive of satisfaction. I pointed out that the cultural level in such places was low.

She would not agree, and snapped: 'There's always the university of life, you know!'

Hardy, like Jude, had to make do with 'the university of life': he mixed, eventually, with royalty, but he never lost his loyalty to the people from whom he came.

Index

157